# Contents



## EXCLUSIVE!



## SPECIAL FEATURE



# the 1983 SCOU... annual



**The Official Cub Scout Annual of The Scout Association**
**Edited by David Harwood**

## COMPETITION



## SPECIAL FEATURE



**THE COVER PHOTOGRAPHS**

**Front:** Anthony Vanderweele and David Nally of the 25th Chingford Cub Scout Pack having great fun during a tug o' war at camp.

**Back:** Alastair Harwood (left) and Keith Weaver of the 1st Frampton Cotterell 'A' Cub Scout Pack exploring during a District Scout Family Camp.

**This Annual belongs to:**



Published in Great Britain by World International Publishing Limited,
A Pentos company, P.O. Box III, Great Ducie Street, Manchester M60 3BL.
Printed in Belgium.
SBN 7235 6646 1.

# JUNK GAMES

**Devised, written and illustrated by Vic Clapham**

**Whatever you do, don't drop litter . . . but before you throw anything away ask yourself 'Could I use it?' . . . This feature gives you some ideas for making games and working models from junk.**

## BEAN-BAG SHUFFLEBOARD

Shuffleboard was extremely popular in the 16th and 17th centuries, when it was known as Shovelboard. In olden times it was played on a small board or table with pieces of money. During the 18th and 19th centuries other forms of the game were developed — one on a large scale in which the board was 30 feet long, and the pieces were heavy weights! Many people this century know the popular shipboard version.

**THE BOARD:**
See diagram, with dimensions. You can use any large sheet of thick cardboard to make it, but it is best to find something like a piece of scrap hardboard that will stand up to wear and tear. Rule the simple lines as shown, and paint them on the board, after rounding the corners with a compass and cutting them away.

**BEAN-BAGS:**
Make eight square bean-bags from any old pieces of cloth, and fill them fairly loosely with dried beans. Mother can show you how. The bags should be quite small, about 9cm x 9cm.

**RULES:**
1. The target board is laid on the ground. A throwing line is marked on the ground 3 or 4 metres from the near end of the board — or less if small children are playing.
2. Usually, two teams of two players per team compete. The first pair toe the line, alternately throwing one bean-bag each, in succession, until all eight bags have been thrown. Their score is added up. The next pair then have their innings. The highest score wins. (A singles match may also be played between two players, each throwing all eight bags in an innings).
3. Scoring: This is done after each innings, when all eight bags have been thrown. Each bag scores in the area in which it has finally come to rest. Any bag touching a line, or hanging even a little bit over the edge of the board, does **not** score.

THE 9 SQUARES SHOULD BE 15cm X 15cm, AND THE END AREAS 15cm X 45cm. THIS GIVES A TOTAL AREA OF 75cm DEEP X 45cm WIDE, LESS CUT-AWAY CORNERS.

## PLANK POWER-BOAT

● *MAKE IT FROM A PIECE OF SCRAP PINE PLANK. PAINT WITH ENAMEL.*

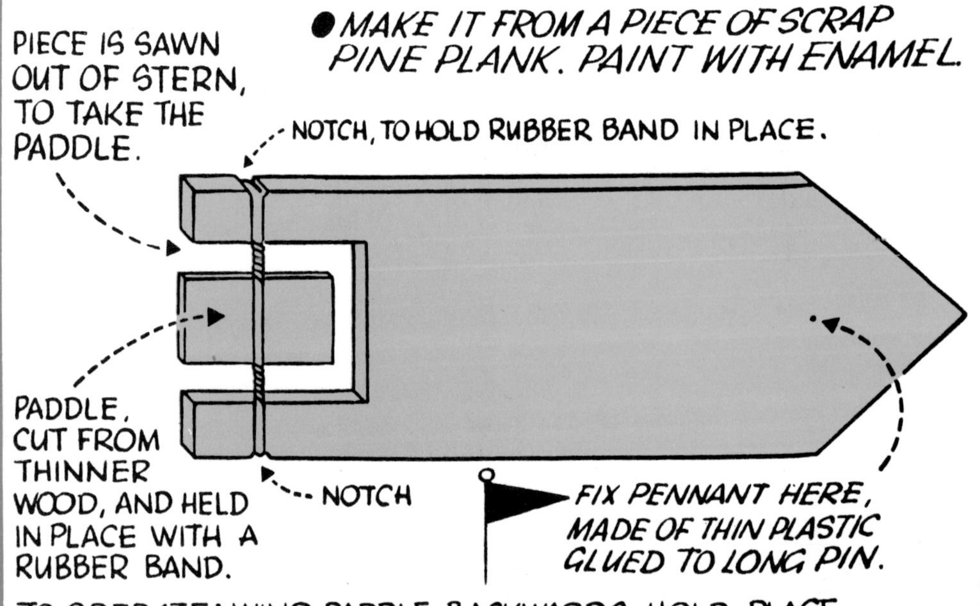


TO OPERATE: WIND PADDLE BACKWARDS, HOLD, PLACE POWER-BOAT IN WATER, AND LET GO! MAKE SEVERAL, AND HOLD POWER-BOAT RACES. AS A GOOD TURN MAKE OTHERS, AS GIFTS FOR NEEDY CHILDREN.

## CAN-BALL

The illustration shows how you can use scrap materials to make this game for children. Type out the following rules and paste them on the back of the board:

**RULES:**

Set up the Can-Ball board at an angle, on its easel. Two players may compete against each other — or teams of two, three or four can be organised. Scoring is according to the numbers under the cans. A throwing line is marked on the ground 1½ to 2½ metres from the board — distance according to the age of the children playing.

Using old tennis balls (or old golf balls, or pine cones, or bean bags) each player throws three balls in succession. The object is to throw the balls into the cans, to achieve the highest possible score. In a match, each player, in rotation, has three 3-ball turns. The winner is the one with the highest score in nine throws (i.e.: three 3-ball turns).

# The 3 R's

**RECOVER**
**RECYCLE**
**RE-USE**

**'Junk Games' has been reproduced, by kind permission, from The Bata Book of 101 THRIFTY IDEAS FOR ENERGY CONSERVATION by Vic Clapham and published by The Boys Scouts of South Africa.**

## FRENCH CRICKET

This is a fast-moving game for boys and girls of all ages. Full of fun and excitement, it can be played by any number from 5 or 6 players up to a couple of dozen, on any piece of open ground.

**EQUIPMENT**

**BAT:**

Cut a wooden bat (see sketch) from a length of scrap pine plank. A standard cricket bat has an overall length of approximately 95cms (38 inches) and a maximum width of 11½cms (4¼ inches) but you can make the bat a smaller "junior" size, to the same proportions roughly. You can file the corners of the handle a little, to give a more comfortable grip, and bind the handle if you wish with adhesive plastic tape of some bright colour; you can also paint the bat a bright colour, after sandpapering it, using a durable enamel.

**WICKET:**

Traditionally, an upturned galvanised iron household bucket was used as a wicket. You can substitute this with a small strong steel drum about 30cms (1 foot) high, and wide enough to stand on when upturned. Paint the drum a bright colour, inside and out.

**BALL:**

An old tennis ball.

**RULES:**

1. A single batsman — anyone — goes in first. He stands on the upturned drum, facing the bowler, bending down a little and holding his bat to protect his wicket, the drum.
2. For the opening ball, the bowler — anyone — stands 5 paces from the wicket. The bowler's object is to hit the wicket with the tennis ball. If he does so the batsman is out, and the bowler takes his place and becomes the batsman standing on the drum.
3. The field of players is spread out in a rough circle all around the wicket, at varying distances. When a batsman hits the ball, the players in the vicinity scramble for it, and the one who gets it becomes the bowler of the next ball. He can bowl swiftly, immediately he picks it up, **standing at the point where he picked up the ball.**
4. If a fieldsman catches the ball, the batsman is also out, and the catcher takes his place as batsman, while the "out" batsman takes the ball and bowls from the point where he himself was caught out. Thus, there are two ways in which a batsman goes out: 1. When his wicket is hit by the ball. 2. When he is caught out.

**And so the game goes on, as long as the players wish.**

# THE FAMILY

by Hazel Addis    Illustrated by Peter Harrison

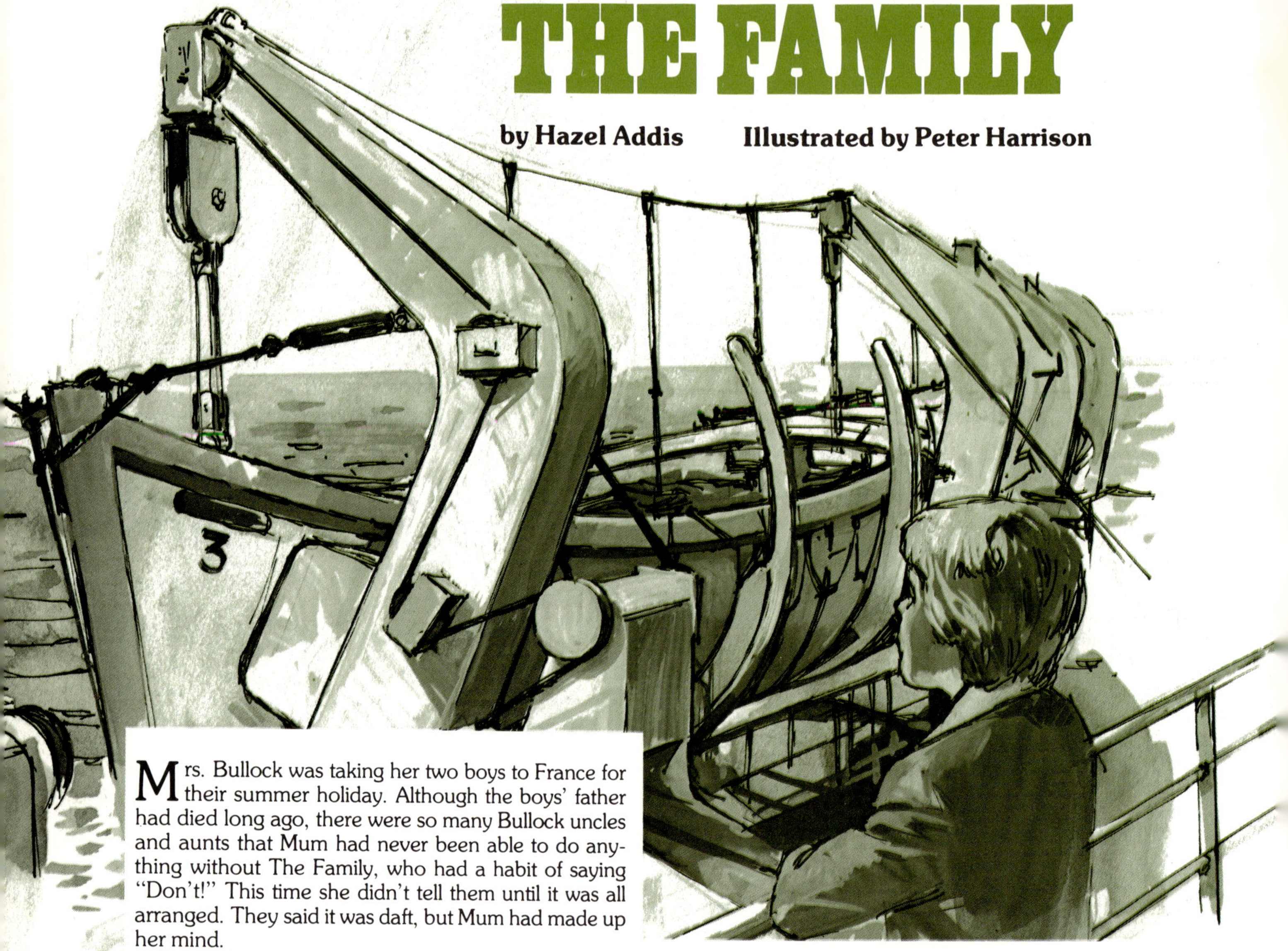

Mrs. Bullock was taking her two boys to France for their summer holiday. Although the boys' father had died long ago, there were so many Bullock uncles and aunts that Mum had never been able to do anything without The Family, who had a habit of saying "Don't!" This time she didn't tell them until it was all arranged. They said it was daft, but Mum had made up her mind.

So off they went, and very exciting it was, crossing the Channel in a ferry and being all on their own. Nobody was seasick, as The Family had said they would be. Tim, who was only seven, hadn't wanted anything to eat on the boat, which was unlike him, but ten-year-old John had enjoyed everything and had raced about the decks even though they were tilting up and down.

Arriving in a foreign country was a real thrill, with everything so different and peculiar. It was rather confusing at the docks where they landed, with everybody shouting at everbody else.

"How they can understand each other, I don't know," said Mum. "Come on, if you can carry a bag each, let's get out of this."

So they went to explore the town before they found the bus for Orger-something, where Mum had booked rooms in a boarding-house. She had written down the address and this was safe in her handbag with their passports and all her French money.

Presently they came to an open square, where there were shops and cafés and lots of people making lots of noise. Some were sitting about at little tables on the pavements, others were dancing and singing to an accordian.

"*Now,*" said Tim, "I'm hungry."

"Something's going on," said Mum. "Let's sit down for a bit and watch the fun." There was a seat under some trees and they were glad to dump their heavy suitcases and have a rest.

More people were crowding round as a sort of procession began moving through the square, led by a banner saying 'FÊTE DE . . .' something or other.

"Funny how they use English words like '*Fête*' and '*Café*'," said John, but he was interrupted by Tim exclaiming: "Look! There's someone buying ice-creams from that stall over there!"

"All right," said Mum. "John, could you go and try to get some? You'd only have to point and hold out a handful of those small coins."

"O.K." said John. "I'll try. Where's the money?"

Where was the money? In Mrs. Bullock's handbag, of course. But where was the bag? She had put it down on the seat beside her, but it wasn't there any more. It must have been knocked over by that crowd of people that had jostled past.

Mum caught her breath on a strangled exclamation, as she looked under and around the seat. The handbag was not there — nor were the suitcases which they had dumped down behind them.

All three Bullocks sprang up with three gasps of horror, staring around. Mum was remembering in the back of her mind some rather rat-faced men she had noticed in the crowd: men who had looked rather suspicious. But there was no sign of them now; nor of the luggage, nor the handbag with all its papers, passports and money.

"No! Oh NO!" Slowly Mrs. Bullock sat down again as though her knees had given way. "It just *can't* have happened," she murmured. But it had. Everything had been stolen.

The next hour was rather like a nightmare and nobody could wake up. What could they do? They didn't know the proper address of the boarding house and had no money to get there anyhow. No money for ANYTHING.

"If only some of The Family was here," sighed Mum. "I'm sure Uncle Joe would know what to do, and Uncle George would say . . ."

" 'Ask a policeman', " said Tim in his Uncle-George voice.

So they did try to ask one or two men in blue uniforms, who might have been bobbies or firemen or postmen for all they knew. It wouldn't have made any difference, because none of them spoke English. All of them spoke much too much French, waving their hands about and finally shrugging their shoulders and walking away.

"Don't worry, Mum," said John, trying to feel as clever as Uncle Joe.

"Don't worry, loves," said Mum. "We'll think of something soon."

But they didn't.

"If only I could send a telegram to The Family," Mum lamented. "I'm sure they could do something somehow, as well as saying it was daft." But you can't send telegrams without any money. You can't do anything except go on sitting under the trees and feeling utterly helpless.

The procession was nearly over. It was getting late and everbody else was going home.

Suddenly John jumped up and Mum cried: "Johnnie, don't go away!"

"You stay there!" shouted John, bossily, just like Uncle Joe. He ran after the procession, for right at the back he had seen some boys marching. They were wearing a uniform which was like his own Cub Scout uniform, and yet different, as everything in France was different.

He was almost sure they were Cubs and yet — they might be some odd Boys' Club, all jabbering French and making John feel an awful fool. They were jabbering all right, for they had just been dismissed, when John caught up with them, but suddenly he knew that everything was going to be all right. Each boy was wearing a brown jersey, a neckerchief and a badge with a *fleur de lis* — the badge wasn't the same as the one on his uniform, but it *was* a Scout badge.

He pushed his way through the mob who were crowding round a tall young man in uniform, saluted him and said: "Excuse me, can you speak English?"

The man smiled while the other boys gaped at him. "Ver' leetle," said the man. "You is Eengleesh Skoot?"

"Yes!" John was glad he was wearing his buttonhole badge and that Akela had told him about all Scouts shaking hands with the left hand. The young Frenchman's left hand was outstretched and John grasped it. "Please, please could you help us?" he said. "We've lost all our money and everything and nobody can understand."

Nor could the Frenchman, for John was trying to tell him all about everything all at once. But he knew something was wrong, as John kept tugging at his left hand, and he allowed himself to be tugged right across the square, until presently he was bowing to Mrs. Bullock.

"Madame," he said politely. "May I aid you?"

It sounded like 'First Aid' and Tim giggled, but Mum said stiffly: "No, thank you," adding to John: "You really mustn't ask strangers for help."

"But he's not a stranger, Mum! He's a *Scout*."

So she explained and the young man sat and listened, looking worried. At last his eyes lit up and he exclaimed: "*C'est ça*! All is now understanding!" After a moment's thought he jumped up, bowing again and saying: "Madame, plis! You com' wit' me?"

He led them down an avenue to a rather grand-looking house and rang the bell. A grey-haired gentleman came to the door, smiled at Akela and listened to his quick burst of French.

Mum interrupted them. "Please don't bother," she said. "We shall be quite all right. Come along, boys!"

But the young Frenchman caught her arm. "Madame, plis! M'sieur Colet is Chef de Skoots in zis town. You are understanding?"

Monsieur Colet was already shaking hands, bowing and smiling as he led them indoors. In careful English he said: "Madame, I am honoured if I may help you in your distress. I beg you treat me as a friend you trust. Your son is a Skoot . . ."

"A Cub Scout, sir," said John.

"*C'est ça*. One of the Skoot Brotherhood, no? What is your name, my friend?"

"John, sir. John Bullock."

The old man started to chuckle. "A small John Bull! Ah, that is indeed marvellous!" Laughter is the same in any language and even Mum was joining in as she sat down and told their story again.

Monsieur Colet shook his head. "It is sad there are thiefs. But now, Madame, this place where you go?"

"Somewhere called 'Orger-something'. I don't know how to pronounce it."

"Augerville, perhaps? A village nearby. And the name of the hotel, or landlady?"

"The letter was signed by a clerk, I think."

"*C'est ça*," said the man. "Now you will please rest content, while I arrange all." He got busy with the telephone and the directory, while they looked round his beautiful room. Presently the old gentleman turned back to them. "All is well!" he cried triumphantly. "Madame Leclerc in Augerville awaits you! You will permit that I escort you in my car?"

"NO!" said Mum. "Thank you very much but we can't go there now. I've no money to pay her."

"But Madame, I . . ."

"I won't have charity from anyone," said Mum firmly. "My family wouldn't like it."

"I understand. But I am very sure your good family will repay me every franc which you must now allow me to lend. Indeed, Madame, this young Skoot belongs to *my* Family. He will trust me, no?"

"Yes," said John. "Of course I will! It really is all right, Mum! Akela is always on about the 'World-wide Brotherhood'. Scout people *are* family, they really are!"

And they were.

The boys made friends with the local Cubs, who were called 'Louveteaux', and they had a super holiday. Of course the Uncles at home got together and sent Mum enough money to repay all she owed and have a good time into the bargain. "Though how The Family will carry on when we get back, I dread to think," sighed Mum. "But I must say Mr. Colet is a lot more polite than Uncle Joe — and I shall tell him so!"

"*C'est ça*!" said the boys, which sounds like 'say sar' and seems to mean 'O.K.'

"Mum?" John went on. "Let's go somewhere abroad again next year. There's 'Family' all over the world!"

Cub Scouts Andy and Chris meet . . .

# OUR NEW CHIEF

**Reporter: David Harwood**
**Photographer: David Stower**

*Major General Michael Walsh talking to Andy and Chris.*

**On the 18th September 1981, The Council of The Scout Association named Major General Michael Walsh, CB, DSO as Chief Scout Designate to succeed Sir William Gladstone, Bt. early in 1982. We asked if two Cub Scouts could interview 'The General' for THE CUB SCOUT ANNUAL. Major General Walsh's reply was immediate: "Certainly!"**

**On Monday 12th October 1981, less than four weeks after the announcement, Andrew Davison of the Tiger Pack and Christopher Kimber of the Panther Pack of the 25th Purley (St. Mark's) Scout Group travelled up to London from Surrey with Dolores Jarvis Smith (Shere Khan of the Tiger Pack) to meet their new Chief Scout and to interview him on your behalf. The boys had done their homework, too, and had given a lot of thought to the questions they wanted to ask.**

**After meeting members of the Editorial Department, Andy and Chris went to the sixth floor of Baden-Powell House where 'The General' welcomed them into his office. Once the 'formal' introductions had been done, the three sat round a table and, with a tape recorder switched on, the interview began . . .**

**One thing I probably ought to tell you first is that I'm not Chief Scout at the moment. As you know, Sir William Gladstone is the Chief at present, and I've been appointed to be the next Chief Scout. I have the title Chief Scout Designate, but that's such a mouthful I think it's best if you just call me 'General'. Now, you're both Sixers, aren't you? Is yours the best Six in the Pack?**

*Andy and Chris:* Yes.

**Well, of course it must be!**

*Chris:* I've been a Sixer for two weeks.

**Have you got some good boys in your Six?**

*Chris:* Not too bad!

**Have you been to camp this year?**

*Andy:* Yes, and I got my Camper's Badge. You have to go to camp twice and cook food outside to get it.

**What cooking did you do? Sausages?**

*Andy:* We cooked sausages, twists and some tomatoes. We ate all ours.

**Well done! Have your Mum and Dad got you to cook at home?**

*Andy:* Yes. One of the tests we have to do for our Bronze Arrow is to invite a friend for a simple meal and wash up. Mum had to write and tell Akela that I'd done it, and then I passed the test.

**It must have been a tasty meal! Have you done any cooking, Chris?**

*Chris:* Not yet.

**Have you been to camp?**

*Chris:* Yes, we went last summer.

**Was that just your Pack or were there other Packs?**

*Chris:* Just ours.

**Like Andy, you've got a good set of Badges, Chris. Let's see what you've got... Sportsman... Athlete . . .**

*Chris:* That's the Musician . . .

**What do you play?**

*Chris:* I sang.

*Our Cub Scout Annual interviewers in action — Andy Davison (left) and Chris Kimber (right).*

**. . . Swimmer — what did you have to do for that?**

*Chris:* I did my Bronze Personal Survival Award which meant doing so many lengths of the pool and several other things. That's the Explorer which I did at camp . . . Book Reader . . . Hobbies and Naturalist.

**You've both done very well. Now, on your other arm you've got other badges . . .**

*Andy:* Yes — the County, the District and the Group. That's the Sixer's Badge. A Second's got one stripe instead of two.

**I was a Cub and so was my brother. We were rivals because we each had a Six. Of course, I**

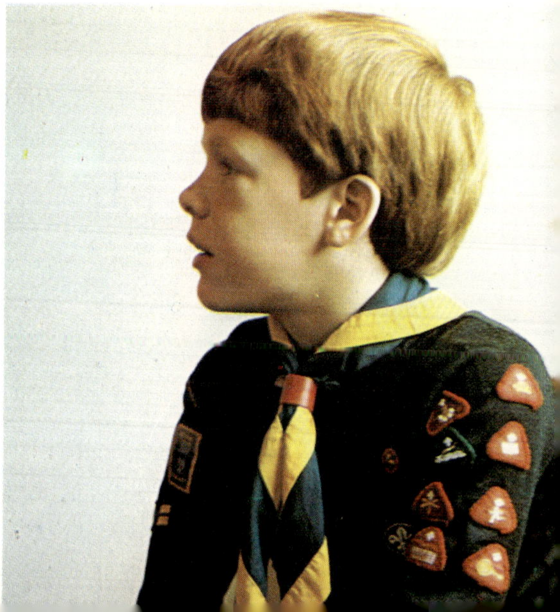

**thought my Six was much better than his, and that used to start fights at home.**

*Chris:* How old were you when you joined the Scout Movement?

**I started as a Cub when I was 8, and then went up to Scouts when I was about 11. At what age do you go up to Scouts these days?**

*Andy:* You take your Link Badge at 10½, and we go up to Scouts a month after we're 11.

**You're going to be 11 soon, aren't you, Andy?**

*Andy:* I'm 11 in December, so I'll go up to Scouts in January.

**You've got a bit longer to do before you go into Scouts, haven't you, Chris?**

*Chris:* Another year. Why did you join the Scouts?

**That's a very good question. I think because everyone got such a lot of fun. Everyone who was either a Cub or a Scout had a lot of fun and a lot of excitement. They got out into the open air and went camping, and tried cooking and all those things. They also did some useful jobs helping people. I think that's very important, to try and help people, particularly people who are not so lucky either because they are physically handicapped in some way so they cannot run around, or old people because old people can have a bit of a difficult time. Do you have schemes in your Pack to help old people?**

*Andy:* We have jumble sales and things, and the money we raise goes to old people's homes. We collected £113 at our last jumble sale.

**That's marvellous, because I think the more you can do things like that, the better . . .**

*Chris:* When you were a Cub what did you enjoy doing most?

**I really liked being out of doors. We had some very nice woods near our meeting place and we used to go and make shelters in them. Then the big day came when we were allowed to sleep in the shelters we'd built. Mind you, I used to find I woke up pretty wet the next morning as my shelter was never very good!**

*Andy:* What sort of school did you go to?

**It was a private school in Harrogate, Yorkshire. There were 60 to 80 boys and it had both a Cub Pack and a Scout Troop.**

*Andy:* What was it called?

**Clifton House School, and the Group was the 10th Harrogate.**

*Andy:* Did you enjoy school when you were there?

**At the time one probably didn't realise it, but looking back, yes I did.**

*Andy:* Do you still have memories of your school?

**Sadly the school closed about 10 years ago, but before that I used to go back when I was on leave.**

*Andy:* What did you do when you left school?

**I went into the Army. Scouting was a great help to me when I became a soldier because you could look after yourself better, live out in the open air, look after your gear and so on.**

*Andy:* Which Regiment were you in?

**I went originally into a London Regiment, The King's Royal Rifle Corps — they're now the Royal Greenjackets. After some years I joined the Parachute Regiment. Another thing I liked — and what you've obviously both done — was sport, particularly athletics and swimming. Do you have sports in your Cubs?**

*Andy:* Yes. About three times a year we go to Downside School which is in Purley and do athletics. We have long jump, high jump, running races, and then we have a cross-country course

# Our New Chief's Background

Major General Michael Walsh was a member of the Clifton House Scout Troop in Harrogate, Yorkshire, as a boy. He gained the rare distinction of gaining the King's Scout Award with Gold Cords which, at the time, was the Scout Movement's highest award for training proficiency and achievement.

When he left school in 1945 he joined the Army as a Private and was commissioned into the King's Royal Rifle Corps (60th Rifles) in 1946. Following graduation from the Australian Staff College and the Joint Services Staff College, he held a succession of appointments in Malaya, Germany, Cyprus, Suez, Aden, Australia, Singapore and the United Kingdom.

In 1978 he became Director of Army Training with responsibility for the policy and direction of the Staff College, Royal Military College of Science and the Royal Military Academy. He retired from the Army in 1981 and lives near Marlborough in Wiltshire. He married in 1952 and he and his wife, Angela, have two daughters, Bridget, who is married, and Gail, who works in London.

'The General' has many leisure interests which include music, the arts and sport. He is an active member of the Church of England. He is a qualified Royal Yachting Association Offshore Skipper and sails a Flying Fifteen. He holds a Private Pilot's Licence. As a qualified parachutist he is President of the Army Parachuting Association, and President of the Army Parascending Association. He was an Army athlete and is a past President of the Army Boxing Association.

which you go round twice. I got the Third Stage of my Athlete's Badge.

**You'll be able to continue that in the Scouts, won't you? And what about swimming? Where do you swim?**

*Chris:* I did mine at a local pool. My brother goes there.

**So you'll be able to do the Royal Life Saving Society's awards when you're a bit older where you're taught to rescue people who are drowning. That's well worth doing.**

*Chris:* Have you been a Pack or Group Leader?

**No. You see, I went from school straight into the Army because it was just at the very end of the Second World War. The war was still on, and you had to go into the Army. I've been so busy since then, I've not had the chance of getting back to Scouting. Now I've left the Army, I shall have the time.**

*Chris:* Why did you want to be the Chief Scout?

**It wasn't a matter of wanting to! The first thing was that I was asked if I'd like to be considered, because there are a number of people who are well qualified to become the next Chief Scout. It's a great honour — a very great honour — to be the head of our Movement in this country. Do you know how many Scouts and Cubs there are in the United Kingdom?**

*Andy:* Over a million probably . . .

**Over half a million — 640,000.**

*Andy:* Are you paid as Chief Scout?

**No. It's a voluntary job, just as it is for most of the Movement. Your Leaders, for example, they're not paid.**

*Andy:* What would you like Cubs to call you?

**When I become Chief Scout . . . 'Chief Scout', I think. But until then, just 'General'.**

*Chris:* When you become Chief Scout, would you like to see any changes?

**I think I've got a lot of learning to do having been away such a long time. I've got to learn about it again, meet lots of people, talk to lots of people. I would like to see as much adventure training as possible where Cubs, Scouts and Venture Scouts have the opportunity to get out in the country, and do as much outside as they possibly can.**

*Andy:* When you become Chief Scout, will you make an organisation after

*The Chief signing autographs for Andy and Chris at the end of the interview.*

Venture Scouts? We've had Cubs, Scouts and Venture Scouts, will you go on from there?

**No. We've got boys from Cubs — as you are — through to Venture Scouts, and I think that's sufficient for the Movement. You see, what we do want is when people finish being Venture Scouts they should come back as Leaders. As you know, lots of Cub Packs have got waiting lists, and the reasons they've got waiting lists is that we haven't got enough Leaders. To those who have been in the Movement we want to say 'Come back now and help run a Cub Pack or a Scout Troop and return something to the Movement.' When you two are grown up, I hope we'll see you back as Leaders!**

*Chris:* Do you make decisions as Chief Scout, or do things just come to you?

**I'm helped by a Committee of wise men, people who've been in or connected with the Movement for many, many years, and so together with that Council we take the decisions. Obviously I can put forward some ideas, but I will be relying a lot on the Council with their advice and experience.**

*Chris:* What exactly do you have to do as Chief Scout?

**First of all let's talk about this great big Headquarters here in London. With the help of the permanent staff and the Committee I've been talking about, I hope to produce a policy and direction, so that we can make decisions and give guidance to the Movement all the way up and down the country. Then the second job is, having made that policy, to go and see if it's working — go round and meet your Leaders and say: 'Is that working? Is that sensible? How does it work in Surrey, in Glasgow, in Cardiff, in Belfast?'**

*Andy:* As a guess, what do you think being the Chief Scout will be like?

**I think it's going to be great fun. It's going to be hard work, too. Most of my spare time will be taken up seeing everybody, and going round meeting boys like you, having a good old chat and, I hope, doing a few things together.**

*Andy:* When you do retire in some years time, will you pick the person to be the next Chief Scout a few months beforehand?

**The selection of a Chief Scout is done by the Committee of the Council of The Scout Association. Obviously I'll take a part in the selection when the time comes. But that, I hope, will be some years yet! . . . Are there any more questions you'd like to ask?**

*Andy and Chris:* Please may we have your autograph?

**Yes, fine! I've got a present for each of you because I think you've done very well with this interview. So here's a Slinger pen for you, Chris, and one for you, Andy. I wish you both well, and lots of luck when you go up into the Scouts.**

*After the interview Andy and Chris were photographed with 'The General' beside the magnificent statue of The Founder which stands at the entrance to B.-P. House.*

# Brazil nut

**Tropical South America** *Tree, 30 - 50m high*

The brazil nut grows on an enormously high tree. This tree, which grows wild, is often found along river banks in Brazil and Venezuela. The brazil nuts we buy from the greengrocer come out of a hard wooden pod. Sometimes there are as many as three hundred pods on one tree. There are between eight and twenty-four nuts in a pod; each pod is about the size of an orange and the nuts are packed inside like the segments of an orange.

# Walnut

**North and South America**
**Europe Asia West Indies**
*Tree, up to 30m high*
*Leaves, 300mm long*

Walnut trees have to grow for many years before any fruit appears. The tall, sturdy trees produce excellent timber for furniture. Craftsmen like using walnut as it resists attack by insects, does not warp, and is very beautiful when polished. The walnut, which is not strictly a nut, is a traditional Christmas food. The nuts can be crushed into oil, which is used in making oil paints for artists, and for making food.

Clarks
Whirligig Theatre
NUTS OF THE WORLD

# Sweet chestnut

**Temperate parts of North America**
**Europe Asia** *Tree, 30m high*

Horse chestnuts and sweet chestnuts are quite separate plants. We roast and eat the fruits of the sweet chestnut tree. Both the horse chestnut tree (conker) and the sweet chestnut tree are very big and beautiful. The May and June countryside is graced by magnificent pink or white 'candlestick' blossom which covers the conker tree. Autumn's colours are enriched by the golden brown leaves of the sweet chestnut.

# Horse chestnut

**Europe** *Tree, 30m high Flowers 300mm high*

Brown shiny conkers are familiar to all of us. They are great fun for children, and a good source of food for wild deer. Vets used both conkers and the bark of the tree for treating horses. People thought that conkers looked like sweet chestnuts, and so conkers became known as horse chestnuts.

# Hazel

**North America Asia Europe**

*Tree, up to 24m high Leaves, 80 - 100mm long*

Our winter hedges and woodlands are softened by the 'lamb's tail' catkins of the hazel. The catkins become wild hazel nuts. They are an important part of the squirrel's food store. Cultivated hazel nuts (filberts) are a traditional part of *our* Christmas food store!
For centuries, woodmen have coppiced the hazel. Coppicing means removing the main trunk so that many straight rods grow from the stump. These rods used to be used for making wattle and daub houses and fences.

# Coconut

**Tropical islands**

*Tree, up to 30m high*
*Leaves, up to 6m long*
*Husk, 300 - 450mm long; 150 - 200mm diameter*

No tropical island is complete without a group of palm trees, and on these palms grow coconuts. The coconuts we see at fairs and in shops have had their outside husks removed. The long fibres on these husks help the coconuts to float across the sea to other islands, where they then grow into new palm trees. Trained monkeys are sometimes used to collect the coconuts. We use the fibres to make doormats. The flesh inside the husk is dried to make desiccated coconut, which is used in cakes and biscuits.

Those of you who saw David Wood's play *Nutcracker Sweet* will remember meeting William the Conker, Kernel Walnut, and their friends Monkeynut, Hazel, Gypsy Brazil and Old Ma Coconut. See if you can find the origins of these nutty characters on this page.

Botanists, scientists who study plants, say that nuts must have one seed enclosed in a wooden shell. This shell does not open completely when ripe. Using this definition, try to discover which items shown here are nuts. You may have some surprises, because some are not!

The sizes of the leaves vary a great deal from tree to tree. The coconut palm leaf may be as long as 6m, the hazel leaf as small as 80mm. On this page each nut, flower and leaf is illustrated accurately, but not to the same scale.

**Do not, under any circumstances, eat any nuts, seeds or berries that you may find growing in the wild. There are many which are poisonous and they will make you very ill.**

*This feature is based on THE CLARKS WHIRLIGIG Nuts of the World Wallchart which was distributed to schools in conjunction with the 1981 tour of David Wood's musical play for children* Nutcracker Sweet *sponsored by Clarks, the children's shoemakers. It was reproduced by Kallaway (Consultants and Management) Limited, designed by Peter Matthews ASAID and illustrated by Pete Robinson AOI.*

# Almond

**North America (California)**
**Mediterranean region**
**British Isles** *(ornamental trees)*

*Tree, up to 7m high*

The streets of many villages and towns are decorated in spring with the pink blossoms of the almond tree. The fruit of this tree, the sweet almond, has many uses. Marzipan, which is made from ground almonds, is often used on Christmas cakes and wedding cakes. Many sweet smelling bath oils and perfumes have almond oil in them. The bitter almonds grow on the white-blossomed almond tree. These produce almond essence for flavouring cakes, and after processing produce the deadly poison prussic acid.

NOW TURN TO PAGE 2
FOR A VERY SPECIAL OFFER!

# Ground nut

## (Monkey nut)

**North and South America**
**Asia West Africa**

*Bush, 2.4m high*

Ground nuts have this name because the seeds ripen underground. The plant pushes the developing seed pod into the ground. This pod contains two or three seeds. Where ground nuts grow in the wild, monkeys and baboons love to eat the seeds, and that is why they are called Monkey nuts. When they are roasted they are called peanuts, and we eat them. Most ground nuts are crushed for their oil. The oil is used in making margarine and soap.

# Cola nut

**West Africa** *Tree, up to 12m high*
*Seedpod, up to 150mm long Leaves, up to 200mm long*

It is surprising to discover that the famous soft drink called Coca Cola is made from a nut. Cola nuts grow on an evergreen tree with leathery leaves. The cola nut grows inside a pod. These pods contain several nuts the size of a horse chestnut. The flesh of the nut is brownish in colour, and bitter to taste. The cola nut is also used in the manufacture of some medicines.

The Pitts Special puts on a fine aerobatic display.

# FLYING HIGH

**written and photographed by Michael Edwards**

Most Cubs would like to fly their own aeroplane, but the possibility of that happening is somewhat remote . . . unless you enter the colourful and exciting world of *model* aircraft.

Flying model aircraft is one of the most popular pastimes. Every weekend, about 100,000 miniature plane enthusiasts head for the hills where the air currents they need to fly their models are found.

Today's model makers have some of the most up-to-date equipment available. This is the age of radio control in which expensive and powerful machines are flown not with the aid of wires, but by radio waves.

Some radio models are so big that they require a Certificate of Airworthiness before they can be flown.

Most beginners do not realise that to fly model aircraft successfully, they must know how real aircraft fly, otherwise they are likely to have a smashed model on its maiden flight.

The best starting place for anyone wanting to take up this hobby is a local model aircraft club. If you do not know of one in your neighbourhood, ask at your local model shop.

It's a very good idea to start with a free flying plane or glider. These models are full of fine detail. They have no moving parts, and have to be made carefully and accurately if they are going to remain airborne.

When Cub Scouts Peter Gauge and Nicholas Hancock of the 1st Southport (Ainsdale) Pack visited a model aircraft display at R.A.F. Woodvale, they were shown the world's largest model Jumbo Jet, which was built by a team of model aircraft enthusiasts from Liverpool. Made to 1/20th scale, the huge model weighs 56 lbs; has a wing span of 12' 6"; cruises at 60 m.p.h. — and cost £1,200 to build.

Your interest and enthusiasm will be boosted if you watch your local club's flying models. The experts make it look so easy as their machines loop-the-loop, but they can do it only because they have put in plenty of practice.

The Shadow, a pulsating jet, is the fastest radio controlled model aircraft in the world, which can fly at 223.5 m.p.h. It was built by a Dutch team. It is launched from this raised trackway which incorporates a powerful caterpult.

This massive Lancaster Bomber model was built to 1/6th scale. It weighs 110 lbs; has a wing span of 18 feet; took over 2,000 man-hours to construct from spruce and balsa; and cost a staggering £10,000. It flies, too!

A cockpit close-up of a 1918 United States Army aircraft.

A Chance Vught Corsair Carrier.

# Britain's Reptiles

by Anthony Wootton

Illustrated by Brian Robertshaw

**Britain is not very well off for reptiles. Only six species — three lizards and three snakes — occur naturally in these islands, and some of them are rare. One reason for this lies in our rather variable climate. Reptiles are cold-blooded which means that, unlike mammals and birds, they cannot regulate their body temperature but have to rely on outside conditions for their rate of activity. If it is warm, they are active enough, but in cold weather they become sluggish. In fact, all of our native species spend the winter in hibernation, perhaps tucked away in a hole or beneath the roots of a tree. Not surprisingly, then, the majority of the world's 6,000 or more reptile species live in the tropics, where the temperature does not vary much.**

**Why some people dislike reptiles, especially snakes, is a bit of a puzzle — especially to the *herpetologist*, or student of the group (the word is derived from the Greek 'crawling thing'). It is more understandable in hot countries, where there are many poisonous species, some of them quite dangerous, but not in Britain. We have only *one* venomous reptile — the adder or viper — and even this handsome snake only bites in self defence, and never attacks first. A reptile's skin is not slimy but dry and smooth, and its tongue is merely a sense organ, concerned with touch, taste and smell. Even a snake's 'slithery' movement is a thing of wonder and beauty: *you* try crawling without using your arms and legs!**

1 and 2. SAND LIZARD (*Lacerta agilis*)

The rarest of Britain's lizards, the sand lizard is mainly confined to parts of Dorset, Hampshire, Sussex, Surrey and Kent, with a few isolated pockets elsewhere. It lives in fairly dry areas, such as sandy heaths, hedgerows, meadows and sand dunes, and grows up to about 20cm long, including tail. In the breeding season, which occurs from about May to July, the male's green coloration becomes very bright (**1**); females are dull by comparison (**2**). Unlike our other two species, the sand lizard lays eggs, usually placing them under stones or in the soil.

3 and 4. COMMON or VIVIPAROUS LIZARD (*Lacerta vivipara*)

Unlike the sand lizard, the common or viviparous lizard's young are born fully formed ('viviparous' means 'live-bearing'). The common lizard is smaller than its relative and prefers slightly damper situations. It is very widespread throughout Britain and feeds on a variety of insects as well as spiders. The blackish or dark brown young are, like their parents, very fast moving. Both the female (**3**) and the male (**4**) like to bask in the sun, especially on old tree stumps, and are very difficult to observe, even with the stealthiest approach.

5. SMOOTH SNAKE (*Coronella austriaca*)

Anyone who sees a smooth snake can congratulate himself on his good fortune, since this species is rare, with a somewhat similar distribution to the equally uncommon sand lizard. It is unique among British snakes in killing its prey (mainly small mammals) by constriction — crushing its victim in its coils, like a python, and then swallowing it whole. In appearance it is more like an adder than a grass snake, and is about the same length, though it never has the zig-zag pattern.

6. VIPER or ADDER (*Vipera berus*)

This is Britain's most widespread snake. The adder is not dangerous to man and never bites unless stepped on or deliberately handled. In fact, it is difficult to get close to one at all without it slithering off into the undergrowth, since it is very sensitive to the vibration caused by footsteps. Especially common in open woodlands, adders feed on small mammals, such as mice and voles, which they kill with their venom transmitted through a pair of fangs in the upper jaw. Vipers are easy to distinguish from grass snakes. They rarely exceed 75cm in length and the dark zig-zag down the back is very distinctive, although there is an uncommon black form which could cause confusion. The adder's young are born fully formed but inside a delicate membrane which the little snakes quickly break. They can kill small animals right from birth.

7. SLOW-WORM (*Anguis fragilis*)

Despite its snake-like appearance, the slow-worm is really a legless lizard. It has remnants of limb girdles attached to its backbone, and also has eyelids, which no snakes possess. Like all lizards, the slow-worm will shed its tail if roughly handled and this, together with its glassy smooth body, probably gave rise to one of its alternative names — 'glass snake'. Another is 'blind-worm', although its vision is good. Slow-worms can be found in all sorts of places where it is sunny and warm and where there is cover to which it can retreat. One of its favourite habitats is railway embankments, where it can be encountered basking in the sun in summer or, in winter, sheltering under stones.

8. GRASS SNAKE (*Natrix natrix*)

Much longer than the adder, extending to a length of about 150cm, the grass snake is easily distinguished by its black and bright yellow collar and general greenish colour spotted with black. The pupils of the eyes are round, whereas the viper's are oval in shape. It lives in the vegetation beneath hedges and also along the banks of rivers, ponds and lakes. It can swim well and often catches newts and frogs (**9**) for food. Like all snakes, its jaws are only loosely attached to the skull, allowing it to swallow large prey. The grass snake often lays its soft-shelled eggs in manure heaps, and the little snakes that emerge sometimes cause concern to gardeners, although they are, of course, completely harmless.

## Key

# WHO WERE THE CHIEFS?

Major General Michael Walsh became the United Kingdom's sixth Chief Scout in the spring of 1982. You can see what he looks like and read about him on pages 9, 10 and 11. Do you know who his five predecessors were? Can you identify the other five men who have led the Scout Movement in the UK from the photographs on this page? Between which dates did each serve as 'Chief'? The answers are on page 63 . . . but don't stop there! Find out as much as you can about these men who helped to make the Scout Movement what it is today.

A

B

C

D

E

# Off to Camp!

by Ron Jeffries

Illustrated by Martin Aitchison

**Going to your first camp with the Cubs? Wondering what you'll need to take and what you'll do when you get there? If so the next few pages will help you, for we are going to answer some of the questions that first-time campers ask.**

**If you have been to camp before, don't turn to another page because we think you'll pick up some tips and ideas to use at your next camp.**

**Mum and Dad will be interested in these pages, too, for they will want to help you to collect your kit together for the great adventure. We are suggesting some things for you to try out before you go to camp: Mum and Dad or an older brother or sister might be able to help you with these.**

## What to take

A few days before you go to camp collect together all the things you want to take. You will then have time to buy or borrow any missing items.

Make your own list and put the things in one place before you start to pack. Spread them out on the floor in a corner of your bedroom and tick each item on your list as you do so.

Sew name tapes on items of clothing. Write your name on sticky tape and fix this to the handle of your mug, on the backs of plates and cutlery.

Plastic bags are useful for keeping things dry at night and to put dirty clothes in.

## Before you go . . .

Here are some things to try out before you go to camp. They will help to make your stay more comfortable — and you'll have more time to enjoy the fun of camping, too.

## Packing

Rucsac, kitbag or holdall — that will depend on what's available. For your first weekend camp with the Cubs a kitbag will do just as well, but if you are able to borrow a holdall or rucsac you will be able to keep your kit tidier and find things more easily.

The secret of packing for camp is to put all the things you will need first on top or in the pockets and the items you won't need immediately towards the bottom.

Pack your 'sleeping' kit at the bottom — sleeping bag, pyjamas and so on. Next put your 'wearing' items — spare clothes that you don't need at the moment. Your 'cleaning' gear — towels, toilet bag — and the things you need for 'eating' will have to come out soon after you arrive in camp, so put these nearer the top. Lastly, your groundsheet for 'keeping dry' and your raincoat, anorak or cape — so that if it rains you can reach them quickly. Put the 'extras' in the pockets.

## Making your bed

If you have a sleeping bag use a sheet bag inside — you can wash the sheet bag when you go home at the end of camp. Your sleeping bag will keep clean for longer. Put your groundsheet down first. Next fold your blanket and put this on top of the groundsheet. Now unroll your sleeping bag. In camp, cold rises from the ground and you need more thicknesses underneath than on top. If your sleeping bag has a hood, practise folding it so that it will fit into its hood.

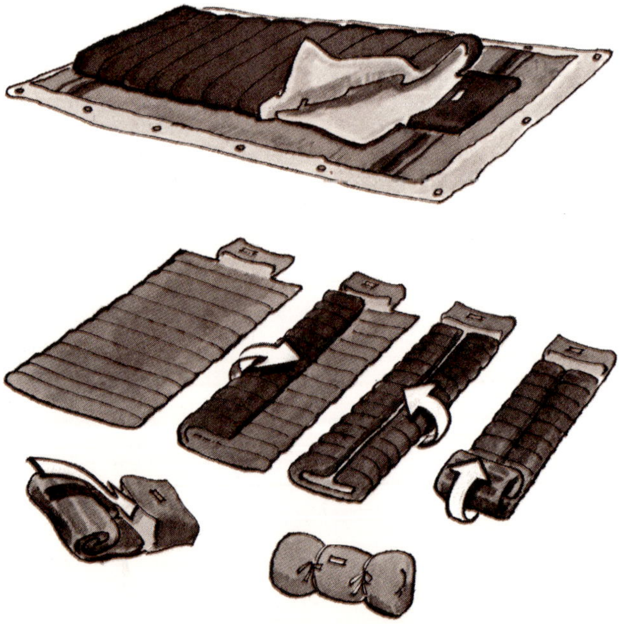

Even if you have your own sleeping bag it's a good idea to learn how to make a bed with blankets and pins — just in case there's an emergency and you need to know how to do this. Start by placing your three blankets on the ground with the sheet sleeping bag on top — then follow the drawings.

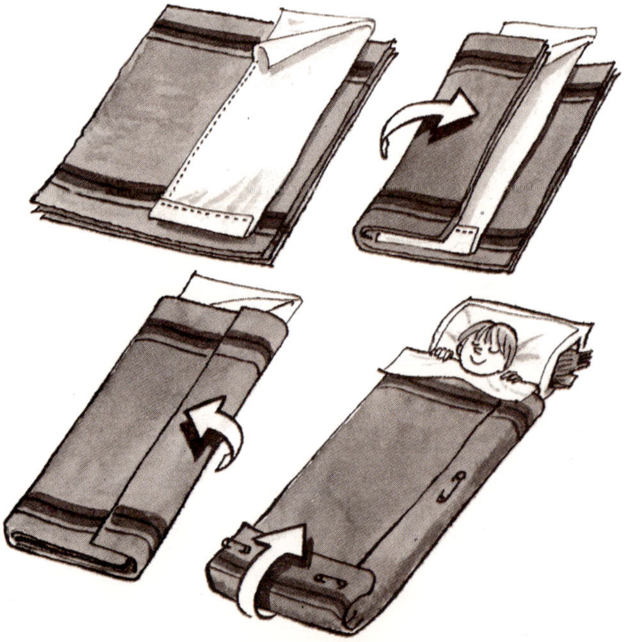

# In Camp

**There are things to do from the moment you get up right through the day until you go to bed at night . . .**

**1** The early morning sun shining through the doors of your tent will wake you up.

**2** The first thing to do is have a good wash — stripped to the waist. Use plenty of clean water and soap — and brush your teeth, too. Then you'll feel fresh and ready for the day's activities.

**3** Breakfast will soon be ready — the Leaders will be cooking this over an open fire or on stoves.

**4** All the Cubs will have their breakfast — outside if it's fine or under dining shelters or in a marquee if it's cold or wet.

**5** Washing up — and everyone does their own plates and cutlery.

**6** Now it's time to help with a few chores around the camp. There's wood to be fetched, water containers to be filled and the kitchen needs tidying after breakfast.

**7** Back to the tents — to get them ready for inspection. If it's fine we pull all the kit outside and hang the groundsheets up to air with the sleeping bags. Akela will come along to make sure that our kit is laid out for inspection and that our uniforms are neat and tidy.

**8**

Now the morning's activities can start! Perhaps we'll have field games or camp sports.

**9**

If it's hot, we'll have a light lunch — and then everyone settles down for the rest hour when we read or play quiet games.

**10**

In the afternoon there might be a hike or we may follow a nature trail. If there's safe water nearby, we could swim before our evening meal.

**11** Dinner — camp food always smells good and we'll be hungry after a full day in camp.

**12** Free-time to explore before we get our tents ready for the night.

**13** Time for the camp fire when we sing as the flames flicker in the dusk, and have a warm drink before we go to bed.

**14** Into our tents and our warm sleeping bags for a good night's sleep under the stars.

# While you're in Camp...

If it's raining or cold and you have to keep your kit inside your tent during the day, here are some tips to keep yourselves comfortable.

Put all your rucsacs, kitbags and so on down one side of the tent. Make sure they don't touch the canvas walls or roof — or the rain will come through. Roll the tent groundsheet back halfway and when you come into the tent walk on the upturned underside of the groundsheet. Take your boots or shoes off as soon as you come inside. Don't touch the walls or roof of the tent with any part of your body or the rain will come through to give you a soaking!

If you get wet, change into some dry clothing as soon as you can. When it's wet or if there is dew on the ground, it's best to wear plimsolls without socks, or gum boots. If you feel cold, put on another sweater straight away. When the sun comes out enjoy it — but be careful. Sunburn and sunstroke can be very painful — so take things slowly until you are used to the sun.

Cooking your own food in camp is fun. Perhaps Akela will let you and the other Cubs make your own tea one afternoon?

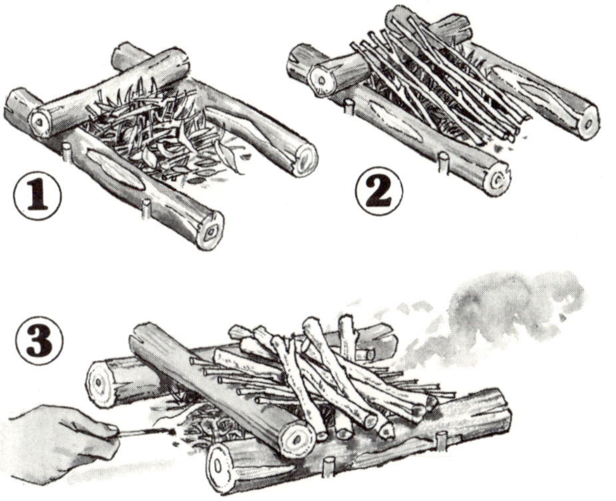


First you'll need to light a fire. Find a place away from undergrowth and trees. If you need to remove the turf, Akela or an older Scout will show you how to do this. Collect some dry wood first — small twigs to start your fire and larger pieces to keep it going. Twigs, cones and pieces of birch bark will act as kindling to get the fire going.

Twists are the camper's bread and you can make them once your fire has been burning for some time and you have a good bed of hot embers. If you try to cook twists in flames, you will end up with a burned, smoky mess — not nice to eat at all! Cut a green stick and peel off the bark. Akela will make sure that you have permission to cut green sticks — don't do this if you are on your own without obtaining permission first. Dry the sap from the stick by holding it over the embers. Mix some flour and water into a stiff paste, roll it out into a sausage shape and then twist it around your stick. Hold this above the embers, twisting slowly all the time so that it is cooked on all sides and right through. Eat your twist while it's hot, spread with butter or jam.

# Our Founder's Simple Faith

DUTY TO GOD

To many people religion is a very complicated thing. But B.-P. had a simple faith. In the early editions of *Scouting for Boys* he put it this way:

> "Religion to me is a very simple thing. It is founded on two things — love God and try to carry out His Commandments; and love and serve your neighbour as yourself."

B.-P. also wrote these words which are not so well known:

> "Many are the names of God, and infinite are the forms which lead us to know Him. In whatsoever name or form you desire to know Him, in that very name and form you will know Him."

Even though the words of the Law and the Promise which B.-P. wrote for the first Wolf Cubs are slightly different from those in the Cub Scout Promise and the Cub Scout Law today, their meaning is the same. When was the last time you really thought about the Promise you made?

Shortly before he died in Kenya on January 8th 1941, B.-P. wrote these lines which carry their own message . . . of his thoughts at the end of his life, and his hopes for young people like you at the beginning of their lives.

*There is a scent of roses on the air,*
*and sweet briar;*
*A rook calls sleepily in the elms*
*nearby in answer to the distant*
*crooning of the dove.*
*A bee hums drowsily by, hiveward*
*bound;*
*All is peace in the home at dusk ere*
*night closes down.*
*She sits with me in the silence of*
*comradeship;*
*Who has shared some of the toil of*
*the afternoon,*
*And the joy of it.*
*It is good to laze, honestly half*
*tired,*
*And to look back down the years*
*and feel*
*That though one has had one's day,*
*It has, in spite of one's limitations,*
*not been an idle one;*
*And that one has enjoyed life to*
*the full,*
*And that, too, one is lucky in being*
*so rich,*
*Rich through having few wants,*
*and fewer regrets.*
*Through an upper window comes*
*the laughing chatter of young*
*folks going to bed;*
*Tomorrow is their day;*
*May it be as happy a one as mine*
*has been;*
*God bless them.*
*As for me, it will be my bedtime*
*soon,*
*And so, Good Night,*
*"Sleep after toil;*
*port after stormy seas;*
*Ease after war; life after death,*
*doth greatly please."*

Based on an article by Vic Clapham in *Veld Lore*, the quarterly wall newspaper for boys, published for the Southern Zone, Africa Region, The World Organisation of the South Movement, by the Boy Scouts of South Africa.

**Illustrated by Stephen Roberts**

# The Many Faces of Baden-Powell

**words by Peter Brooks**

**illustrations by Roger Hall**

Part of a portrait of Lord Baden-Powell of Gilwell, painted by David Jagger, which now hangs in the World Scout Bureau, Geneva, Switzerland.
© The Scout Association of the United Kingdom.

Robert Stephenson Smyth Baden-Powell, 1st Baron Baden-Powell of Gilwell, was an extraordinary man. His life falls into two halves, in each of which he achieved success, distinction and world-wide fame. We're not going to tell his life story here, but instead we're going to let you glimpse some aspects of this very remarkable person.

He was . . .

. . . A SOLDIER

Perhaps the best known of B.-P.'s Army exploits was during the Boer War with his defence of the South African town of Mafeking against a besieging force of more than nine thousand Boers. B.-P.'s one thousand strong garrison held out for 217 days until a relief column arrived. It had managed to hold out only through the tactical, cunning and resourceful leadership of B.-P.

. . . A HUSBAND, A FATHER AND A GRANDFATHER

Although he married quite late in life (at the age of 54) B.-P. and his wife Olave had three children — Peter, Heather and Betty — who would give the Baden-Powells nine grandchildren.

. . . AN ACTOR AND AN ENTERTAINER

Throughout his life B.-P. was a natural entertainer. His flair for amateur dramatics led him to play many parts in different plays and sketches: some of the roles he played were serious, but most were funny. Here you can see him made up to play the part of Wun-Hi in *The Geisha* in 1897.

. . . AN ORATOR

Few men have the talent to be really great public speakers but B.-P. was one man who had this gift. He could have an audience of thousands hanging on his every word. He could stir them, move them and unite them. Each person listening felt that the great man was speaking directly to him or her personally, that he understood their problems and their hopes, and that he was their special friend.

. . . A CAMP LEADER

Brownsea Island 1907 . . . so much has been written about this historic camp, but it *was* B.-P.'s brainchild. At the time he was already 50 years old, yet it was to be the start of his second career as the Founder of Scouting and Guiding, and would lead to his becoming a national hero for a second time.

. . . A PHOTOGRAPHER

In his later years B.-P. became a keen movie maker. Wildlife was just one of his favourite subjects. On one occasion he filmed several lions in the wild in Africa from a distance of just fifteen feet.

. . . A HUNTER

B.-P.'s talents as a hunter started developing while he was still at school where he would go into the out-of-bounds 'Copse' to set snares in which occasionally he caught a rabbit or a hare. He learnt, by experience, to skin, clean and cook his catch. He realised that his cooking fire would have to be smokeless, otherwise it would give his position away to any teachers who might be patrolling nearby. Hunting also formed a part of his Army life: this picture shows him on an expedition in Swaziland in 1889.

. . . A FISHERMAN

Fishing was one of B.-P.'s favourite ways of relaxation. Rivers which required more than usual care and courage, and where he could be entirely alone, provided the challenge that he wanted. He founded the Wey Fly Fishing Association.

. . . A TEACHER

B.-P. was a great teacher. He had the knack of being able to explain things in a way that could be understood by all boys whatever their background.

. . . AN ARTIST

Drawing, sketching, painting and modelling were also among B.-P.'s talents. His water colour paintings in particular show a deep understanding and love for Africa, the continent in which he spent much of his life. B.-P. was ambidextrous, so he could write, paint, draw or sketch equally well with either hand.

. . . A SPORTSMAN

Throughout his life B.-P. kept himself fit. Even at the age of eighty he was still doing daily exercises. One of his main sporting interests was polo. In his Army career he was a member of his regiment's team. As a young officer he would break in and train polo ponies to supplement his Army pay.

. . . A SECRET AGENT

B.-P.'s 'spying' activities are the subject of many stories told to Cubs and Scouts. Perhaps one of the best known of his exploits was the time when he dressed as a butterfly enthusiast and roamed the hills overlooking the enemy's fortifications. Although sentries and patrols stopped him several times, he acted out the part, talking about the specimens he had seen and showing them his sketchbook. What the soldiers didn't notice, however, was that in one of the butterfly drawings he had concealed the size, shape and weaponry of the fort they were guarding! Observation, camouflage and stalking were all ingredients for success, and B.-P. would later emphasise the importance of these in Cub and Scout training . . . and we still do today.

. . . A HORSEMAN

Horses played a very large part in his life. Much of his Army career was in a cavalry regiment, and horses were the main form of transport when he served in India and in Africa.

. . . A STORYTELLER

Every evening at that historic camp on Brownsea Island the boys would gather round the camp fire and B.-P. would relate tales of his Army experiences to a spellbound audience. A year later, in 1908, at the first official Scout camp at Humshaugh, B.-P. again captivated his young audience with his skill in storytelling.

. . . AN ANIMAL LOVER

All animals, but particularly dogs and horses, always held a very special place in B.-P.'s affections.

. . . A WRITER

*Scouting for Boys* and *The Wolf Cub's Handbook* are the two books which B.-P. wrote which have a special significance for Scouting, but he also wrote a number of other books and pamphlets which, even now, make interesting reading.

IN THE LAST few years THE CUB SCOUT ANNUAL has been behind the scenes at many interesting places. In 1977 we watched Concorde being built; in 1979 we went inside The Magic Circle in London; in 1980 we took a close look at British Rail's High Speed Train; in 1981 we spent a day seeing how guide dogs for the blind are trained. Last year Cubs found out how maps are made at Ordnance Survey's Southampton Headquarters and discovered how Team Lotus built their Grand Prix racing car. For each feature we've always taken along Cub Scouts to ask the questions and do the investigating. How do we decide what features to do? Usually we follow up ideas sent by you, the readers of the Annual, from your 'suggestions for future features' on the Competition Entry Form. That's just what happened this year. A number of Cubs asked to know more about lifeboats and the lifeboat service.

# This is the LIFEBOAT SERVICE

**by David Harwood**
**photographs by Alastair Mulhearn**

In the summer of 1981 four Cub Scouts made their way to the harbour at Troon, a small town which lies on the west coast of Scotland on the Firth of Clyde, mid-way between Ayr and Irvine. It's well known for its golf courses, five of which are of championship standard. It's a holiday resort with an old harbour which serves a small fishing fleet, a busy modern shipyard, and a recently developed yacht marina which was opened by round-the-world yachtsman Robin Knox-Johnston in 1978.

David Mackay, aged 10, and Andrew Trotter, almost 11, didn't have to travel as they both live in Troon. Both belong to the 28th Ayrshire Scout Group — Andrew being the Black Sixer of the Gladstone Pack, and David the Second of the Rowallan Pack's Green Six. They knew that Troon had a lifeboat, but hadn't been to the lifeboat station before. Stuart Wallace lives in Balerno, a few miles south of Edinburgh, where he is the Second of the White Six in the 42nd Midlothian - Currie Kirk Pack. The fourth Cub investigator was Alastair Harwood of the 1st Frampton Cotterell 'A' Pack near Bristol.

As arranged, the four boys arrived on the quay by the harbour just after 10.00 a.m. At the corrugated iron building beside the small dry dock (which, incidentally, was built long ago for repairing the Royal Navy's wooden sailing ships) the boys were met by Ian Johnson, the Troon lifeboat's Coxswain/Mechanic. He led the boys through the equipment store to an inner room which houses the radio 'shack' and acts as the crews' rest room, office and shop.

The lads' task was to find out as much as they could about the lifeboat service, and they wasted no time in getting down to business! They asked Mr. Johnson lots of questions . . .

**How long have there been lifeboats?**
A man called Sir William Hillary founded the Royal National Lifeboat Institution in 1824, so it's the oldest national lifeboat service in the world. Before then there were several individual lifeboat societies around the coast, but Sir William (who was a lifeboatman himself) felt there was a need for some kind of national organisation.

**What does the R.N.L.I. do?**
It's main aim is the saving of life at sea. We provide, on call, a permanent service to cover search and rescue requirements up to 30 miles out from the coasts of the United Kingdom and the Republic of Ireland.

**How long has there been a lifeboat at Troon?**
The local people in Troon asked for a life boat and in 1871 a boathouse was built on the main street in the middle of Troon. Our first lifeboat was a pulling and sailing boat. It was towed to the beach on a trailer drawn by horses. As you can imagine, this took quite a long time, and it was sometimes difficult to launch. So it was decided that the lifeboat should be kept afloat all year round. The boathouse was sold to the county council. We moved here in 1905 . . . though *I* wasn't born then! In 1929 Troon got its first lifeboat with an engine.

**How many lifeboats have you had?**
Our present one — The Connell Elizabeth Cargill — is our seventh . . .

**How did it get its name?**
A Mr. W. A. Cargill gave it to us in 1968 in memory of his mother.

**How much did it cost?**
More than £34,000 – and that was in 1968.

**It must cost a lot of money to run the lifeboats.**
It does! This year it will be more than £14 million!

**Doesn't the council or the government pay for your boats and things?**
No. You see the R.N.L.I. is a charity whose money comes from voluntary contributions and donations from people, organisations, companies and so on. In 1974 the Scouts ran a nationwide campaign and raised more than £103,000 to buy a 44-foot Waveney Class lifeboat for Hartlepool. It was officially named 'THE SCOUT' by The Queen in 1977. Today a Waveney lifeboat costs more than £270,000 to build.

**What's your lifeboat like?**
Ours is a Waveney. It's being overhauled at the moment, so you won't be able to see it, but the relief one we have is also a Waveney, and we'll go over that a bit later.

**How many lifeboats are there?**
We've an active fleet of some 260 boats, with a relief fleet of about 60 more.

**How many different types of lifeboat are there?**
Ten, ranging from 16 feet to 70 feet in length. We build to four main designs now — the 52-foot Arun, the 44-foot Waveney, the Atlantic 21 and the 16-foot inflatable which is often called the 'Inshore Lifeboat'.

**Why are there different designs of lifeboats?**
It depends on what the coast is like. Some designs of large lifeboat can only lie afloat, others are particularly suitable for slipway launching and for working among rocks or sandbanks. The individual needs of a station are carefully considered before a new lifeboat is allocated to it. Inflatable lifeboats were introduced in 1963 to deal with the increasing number of casualties close to the shore, but they're not suitable for the worst weather conditions.

**Why did you join the lifeboats?**
I've always liked the sea. I was born and grew up in Troon. I went into the Merchant Navy when I left school. I came out of the Merchant Navy in 1970 and joined the R.N.L.I. full time, working for several years in south-west England. My first appointment was at Clovelly and then I went to Portpatrick as the Coxswain/Mechanic. I became Coxswain/Mechanic here in April 1979.

**Are you paid?**
Yes. Usually the only full-time paid member of the crew is the mechanic, but in some cases — like me! — I'm the coxswain as well. There are two completely full-time crews at Humber in Yorkshire where the men live on an isolated peninsula, and at Clovelly in Devon where there's a cruising lifeboat.

**Are the other men paid?**
Not really, no. They only get a little compensation for loss of earnings which amounts to £3 for the first hour on service and £1 an hour after that.

**Coxswain Ian Johnson shows the boys the equipment in the radio shack. The telephone is a vital link for both incoming and outgoing calls. The radio enables an operator to talk to the Clyde Coastguard, to 'listen in' to ships' broadcasts, and to keep in touch with the lifeboat when it is at sea.**

**The boys looking at the Silver Medal of the R.N.L.I. which was awarded to Mr. Johnson 'in recognition of his courage, leadership and fine seamanship' when the Troon lifeboat rescued the five-man crew of the Dutch dredger *Holland I* on the 12th September 1980. The other five members of the crew on that launch were each awarded the Institution's Silver Medal Service Certificates for their part in the rescue.**

**Stuart tried on a lifejacket for size – later in the day he would wear one 'for real'.**

**THE EQUIPMENT ROOM. Each crew member has a set of weatherproof clothing – fluorescent orange bib and brace trousers; jacket; boots; a safety helmet and a lifejacket. Each lifejacket is secured by straps and inflated by its own compressed air bottle. It has a personal lifeline which will clip to lines on the lifeboat, a whistle to attract attention, and a sea water-activated battery which powers a light which can last for up to 18 hours and is visible at half a mile. On the left hand wall you can see the plaques on which all the lifeboat station's service launches are recorded. The maroons are stored in the red boxes under the plaques.**

Mr. Johnson wheeled out one of the heavy mortar boxes on a trolley. It's from the mortar box that a maroon is fired. A maroon is like a huge firework with a long fuse.

**When do you start work?**
This isn't a job with regular hours, but I usually get here at about 9.00 a.m. The boat has to be maintained in tip-top condition so that when it *is* needed, it's fully operational. Whenever the boat goes out — whether it's a practice launch or a real emergency — I have to clean the whole boat and service the engines. I look after this building and its equipment, too. There's always plenty to do.

**How many crew members are there?**
There are ten of us at present as well as a shore attendant. When we go on service there are usually five in the crew. The Honorary Secretary is shore based, but he and his helpers are a very important part of the team because they provide hot drinks, food and so on when we get back, raise money, and give support in many ways.

**Does everyone in the crew have something to do with the sea?**
No! While some lifeboatmen are fishermen, none are at Troon. We've an assistant manager of a ships' chandlers; a production manager; a tractor driver and a rigger from the shipyard; a sawyer; a diesel fitter; an engineer on a tug; an air traffic controller and a Post Office engineer . . .

**Who can join the crew, then?**
The short answer is any man who is physically fit, but there are some women in the crews of inflatable lifeboats. Everyone has to pass a Board of Trade eyesight test. We meet regularly twice a week on Monday evenings and Saturday mornings, so it's quite a commitment and, of course, we can be called out at any time. To be sure that a new member likes us and we like him there's a trial period of six months. It's most important that we get on with each other and work as a team.

**Does the crew have special training?**
Not as such, no. They learn from practical experience. Although one of the crew is the 'official' first aider when we're at sea, all our crew are qualified first aiders.

**What was your most exciting launch?**
I'm not sure whether exciting is quite the right word! Certainly the most perilous one I've been on was when we went out to a Dutch dredger in September 1980 in a Force 10 gale with 20-foot waves. On our way to the dredger a huge wave broke over the lifeboat, rolling her over so that the side of the wheelhouse was almost in the water. We had to make five separate approaches, and on three occasions the lifeboat crashed hard against the side of the dredger as it rose and fell 15 feet — that's about the height of a two-storey house from the ground to the gutters. We rescued the five people from the dredger.

**Were you frightened?**
Not at the time, no. In fact whenever we launch the lifeboat we never know what to expect. There's so much to do that there just isn't time to stop and think of ourselves and what personal risks we might be taking. But when you get back and begin to relax and look back on what actually happened — and what *might* have happened — I must admit that I do sometimes wonder how we managed it. The sense of relief at having successfully completed a mission is mixed with feelings of fear. And then we're not always successful . . . . When the sea is angry, with huge waves and high winds, and you think how small and relatively helpless we must have been then, yes, I do feel frightened.

The Coastguard Service is usually the first to hear about a casualty at sea. They may have picked up a MAY DAY radio broadcast, or have been alerted by a member of the public dialling 999. H.M. Coastguard co-ordinates all search and rescue work at sea (including other ships, Royal Navy and R.A.F. helicopters and lifeboats) so it is the Coastguard who contacts the Honorary Secretary of the lifeboat to request their assistance. The lifeboat crew are alerted by maroons and/or the telephone, or (in some cases) bleepers are used. In this picture Ian Johnson is showing (*from the left*) Alastair, Andrew, David and Stuart a maroon ready for firing. In a real emergency he would light the fuse and 'get out of the way fast'. The maroon rockets up to 1000 feet where a green flare lets off an explosive charge which makes a huge bang. Each maroon costs £18, and generally two are sent up.

It was almost time for the crew to show the Cubs what happens when the maroons do go up. Mr. Johnson radioed Clyde Coastguard to advise them of the practice launch.

**What happens when the lifeboat is launched?**

There are three main ways of launching a lifeboat — down a slipway, from a carriage which is pushed across the beach by a waterproofed tractor, or by mooring the boat in a harbour or a river estuary. Ours is moored on the other side of this building. We've arranged something rather special for you. A full crew are coming during their lunch hour to show you exactly what happens. Then we'll take you out to sea on an exercise. After lunch you can have a guided tour of the boat . . .

For the next couple of hours the boys had the time of their lives. The photographs and captions tell the story of what they saw and did. When the time came for them to leave they were tired, but they each took away with them memories of a day they will never forget.

**This is the LIFEBOAT SERVICE**

# WHEN THE MAROONS GO UP . . .

1. Within minutes of the maroons being fired, the crew members arrive in their cars . . .

2. . . . run into the station to get into their gear . . .

3. . . . make their way across the dry dock's lock gates . . .

4. . . . and go onto the boat or stand by to cast off.

5. Coxswain Ian Johnson started the engines and took command from his seat in the wheelhouse. He gave orders to his crew over the intercom . . .

6. . . . and the boat reversed out of her berth before making her way to the narrow harbour entrance. This whole sequence took less than seven minutes!

7. The crew brought the boat back to her moorings.

8. The four Cubs put on lifejackets and went aboard.

9. Soon the lifeboat had cast off again, and passed through the harbour entrance to the sea. Coxswain Johnson now opened the throttle of the powerful engines and the boat surged forward, the bow cutting through the waves. The boys stayed in an area behind the wheelhouse to experience the speed and manoeuvrability of the boat . . .

10. . . . and to watch the crew practise such drills as 'man overboard' (using a fender) . . .

11. . . . 'rescue from a smoke-filled compartment' with one of the crew wearing breathing apparatus going to the assistance of an unconscious casualty . . .

12. . . . and 'emergency tiller drill' whereby the boat can be steered manually from the stern if the Coxswain's wheel is out of action.

# INSIDE THE LIFEBOAT

**THE RADIO COMPARTMENT is equipped with VHF radio, a direction finder, radar and an echo sounder. The echo sounder not only gives the depth of water at a particular point, but will produce a trace to give a profile of the seabed over which the boat has passed.**

**IN THE WHEELHOUSE — Coxswain Johnson explains some of the many instruments including alarms, gauges, switches and the compass which, Mr. Johnson said, 'is our oldest but most important piece of equipment.'**

**Alongside the radio is the chart table on which a large scale Admiralty chart is mounted. The chart gives details of the seabed and coastline so a position can be pinpointed or a course plotted, just as a map is used to find the way on land.**

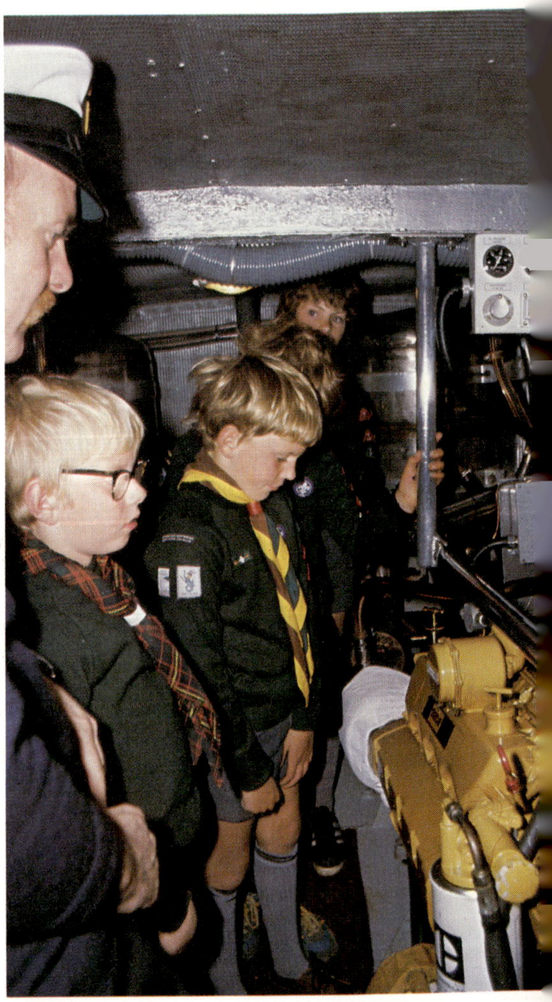

**Down in THE ENGINE ROOM is was quite dark and very warm. The twin 204 hp Caterpillar diesel engines, which give this lifeboat a top speed of 14 knots and a range of 200 nautical miles at full speed, were still hot after the practice exercise. Everything was spotlessly clean, but as soon as the boys had left for home, Mr. Johnson would have to wash down the boat and check over the engines and equipment to ensure the lifeboat was fully operational. A request to launch might come later in the day, the next day, the following week... he wouldn't know when, but whenever it was, he, his crew and the lifeboat would be ready to go.**

## POST SCRIPT

A month or so after our visit, David Mackay's mother wrote to me... "It must have surprised you that we knew so little about the lifeboat service in general and our 'own' vessel in particular. I'd always thought the crew had enough to think about without small boys. On our visit I learned how approachable they were and how kind and understanding to the youngsters. As a result our two Packs have launched a small fund-raising compaign, and we are beginning an association with the lifeboat service...

"At 4.00 a.m. last Sunday morning we were awakened by the maroons. There was a howling gale and driving rain and it was still pitch black. It brought home to David – and me – just what is really involved when a lifeboat is called out."


## ACKNOWLEDGEMENTS

**THE CUB SCOUT ANNUAL** *gratefully acknowledges the help of the Headquarters of the Royal National Lifeboat Institution (R.N.L.I.), Poole, Dorset; the Headquarters of R.N.L.I. Scotland in Edinburgh; and the crew and members of the Troon Branch of the R.N.L.I., particularly Ian Johnson, without whose co-operation this feature would not have been possible.*

# British Wildlife in DANGER

**Written and illustrated by Peter Harrison**

**Wildlife in Britain has been on the decline for centuries. As industry developed and expanded, so towns sprawled across the land. Farming became more intensive to feed the country's growing population. Vast woodland areas were felled to supply the fuel for industrial expansion and to increase the acreage for food production. Slowly at first, but with gathering speed, our native wild life's natural habitats have been destroyed . . . and more destruction is taking place.**

The OSPREY was thought to have become extinct in Britain, but in 1954 a pair nested again in Scotland. The Osprey is still very rare, but with careful protection, it is beginning to breed again.

As streams and rivers became more and more polluted with industrial and building developments, so the OTTER's territory was disrupted and reduced.

With changing harvesting methods and the use of pesticides the HARVEST MOUSE is under threat as its food supplies are being destroyed.

SNAKES HEAD FRITILLARY is a very rare plant, and its flowers should never be picked.

FROGS and TOADS need clean ponds in which to breed. As natural ponds are filled in or become polluted, so garden ponds are becoming more and more important for their survival. Both are good friends to the gardener as they eat insects.

Spraying wasteland and roadsides with herbicides has destroyed the BUTTERFLIES' food sources and the places in which they can lay their eggs.

The RED DEER has adapted to a moorland and mountain habitat. Man has always hunted them by stalking, with pack hounds and the gun. Firearms for killing wild birds and animals have been in general use since the end of the sixteenth century.

**The POLECAT, although a predator of snakes and vermin, is trapped and destroyed because it also kills poultry.**

The RED SQUIRREL has been affected by periodic population declines, but it is probably not driven off by the grey squirrel, as is often thought.

We often hear about sea pollution caused by industrial waste, sewage and oil. However, when detergents are used to 'clear' these, they can themselves be harmful to many species of inshore wildlife.

**BADGERS are gassed in some parts of the country as it is believed that they pass on disease to cattle.**

Modern farming methods have taken away the LIZARD's and the ADDER's natural habitats. Pesticides have eradicated many of the lizard's sources of food.

In some areas the FOX is being destroyed as a predator of poultry and because it is regarded as a general nuisance. It is becoming a suburban creature and can often be seen in and around towns.

**It is in Man's interest to look after his own species. This is not selfish but, at the same time, he must make sure that in so doing he does as much as he can to secure the survival of other species and their habitats.**

# An introduction to TRACKING TRAILS AND SIGNS

**illustrated by Brian Robertshaw**

Tracking is an exciting and enjoyable activity whether you are the one laying the trail or the one following it. However, just as you need to understand the other person when you are having a conversation, so those who lay a trail and those who follow a trail must use a 'language' which both know and understand.

The illustrations on this page give you an idea of some of the signs you can use.

THE WHIFFLE-POOF is an idea from the Boy Scouts of America. It is a log or other piece of wood into which nails have been driven all the way round, with about 2 inches sticking out like spikes. Screw in an 'eye' at one end and attach a thin rope. You can drag the whiffle-poof over the ground and make a continuous trail which will give you excellent training in tracking.

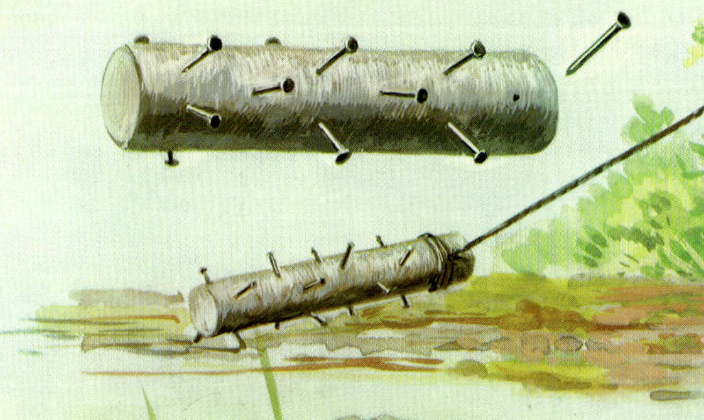

You can use a variety of materials to make a trail: sticks, stones, grass and leaves. Construct the signs so that they can be clearly 'read'. Always remember that the last person following a trail should remove the signs to avoid confusing others who might lay a trail along part of the same route at a later date.

# Magnificent Moths

**written and photographed by Michael Edwards**

I expect that some of you may have cared for caterpillars which you found in your garden or caught scurrying across a country lane. You may have put them into a box or a jar with some food and waited for them to change into a butterfly or a moth.

Cub Scouts from the 1st Farrington Pack in Lancashire have been keeping caterpillars too, but these are rather special caterpillars as they become some of the largest and most exotic moths.

With expert help, the boys obtained moths' eggs from many different countries to study the insects' life cycles, some of which take up to two years.

Moths go through four stages of growth — egg, caterpillar, chrysalis and winged moth. The colours and patterns of these moths are weird and wonderful and have to be seen to be believed.

From the photographs on this page and the next, you will see that the Cubs had a very interesting time studying the insects.

You could try and rear some moths or butterflies yourself. Start with British insects. Only when you have had success with our moths and butterflies should you consider foreign varieties, as the latter need extra warmth and careful feeding to reach the winged stage. Do get an adult to help you!

**Unlike most butterflies, large moths are relatively slow creatures on land, and quite tame too. These Robin Moths from North America were very friendly towards Nicholas Wilding. While taking this photograph (unknown to us at the time) the female moth was laying her eggs on his scarf!**

**It's a good idea to keep a photographic record of a project like this. Roger Kay is taking a light reading while Simon Weedy is checking the moth's position through the camera's viewfinder.**

**Moisture is vital to a moth in the chrysalis stage. If the cocoon containing the chrysalis isn't moistened, the moth may be unable to break out. Temperature is very important for some moths, too. A caterpillar's eating rhythm is controlled by temperature. The Cubs discovered that the higher the temperature, the faster the larvae ate.**

**A Japanese Owl Moth is beautifully patterned in browns, yellows and creams. Notice the two 'eyes' on the upper wings: the under wings also have 'eyes'.**

This striking caterpillar with four twisted horns growing out of its head (there are three at the tail) will eventually become a Japanese Owl Moth. In Britain the larva of this moth will feed on the leaves of ordinary privet.

A caterpillar sheds or sloughs its skin four of five times before becoming a chrysalis. The Japanese Owl Moth shown here has shed its final skin towards the tail (left) and a soft, bright green pupa is the result. If disturbed at this stage the moth will die. This species always pupates in the ground. After several days, the outer covering of the pupa will darken and harden: this happens in May and the moth emerges the following March.

A North American Robin Moth shows off its large wings which have a span of 13 cms. Its caterpillar has blobs of yellow and orange like sealing wax along its body. In Britain, this caterpillar likes to eat hawthorn.

This fearsome creature is the larva of the Privet Hawk Moth. It is a British species and an ideal one for the beginner to study. Look for them on privet hedges in July.

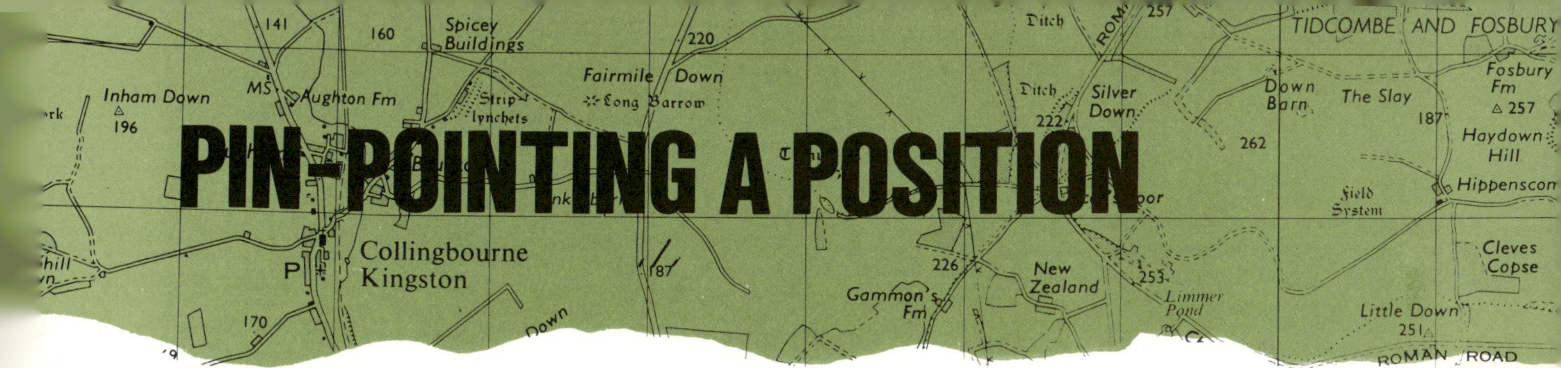


# PIN-POINTING A POSITION

WITH ORDNANCE SURVEY's National Grid, Britain has a unique reference system which enables a place to be located on a map or plan easily, quickly and accurately. All modern O.S. maps and plans carry the National Grid which is a series of squares. The sides of the grid squares are in multiples of the international metre.

Each 100 kilometre square is designated by two letters (see Fig. 1), but for most users it is more usual to state the sheet series and number rather than the 100 km. square letters. On 1:50,000 and some larger scale maps you will find a series of two-figure numbers along all the sides and the whole sheet is overlaid with a grid of squares. Each side of each square is 1/100th of the larger 100 km. square, so each square represents an area 1 km. square! If you look at each corner of a sheet you will see there is one figure before and three 'O's after the two-figure number (see Fig. 2). The first little number represents the number of the *100 kilometre* square (but as we've explained, the 100 km. square is now designated by two letters when used to give a reference.)

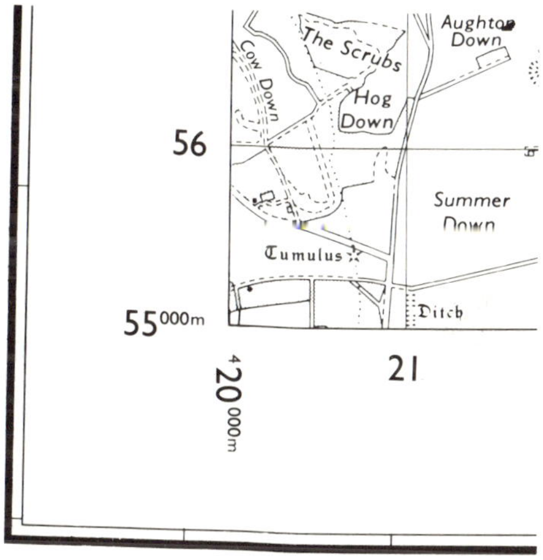


Fig 2

The two-figure numbers which are printed along the edges of the sheet run consecutively from WEST to EAST along the top and bottom margins, and from SOUTH to NORTH in the side margins. Look at Fig. 3, which is part of a map, and we'll show you how to pin-point a position. We've chosen Kintbury Station.

* First take the WEST edge (left hand side) of the kilometre square in which Kintbury Station is located and read the figures printed at either end of the line in the north (top) or south (bottom) margin. *This is called the EASTING.*

The station is in the square to the east of the line 38.

* Second take the SOUTH edge (bottom) of the kilometre square in which Kintbury Station is located and read the figures at either end of the line in the west (left) or east (right) margin. *This is called the NORTHING.*

The station is in the square to the north of the line 67.

THUS THE STATION IS IN THE SQUARE 38/67.

But this reference does not pin-point the position of the station within the square. We need to be more accurate so we sub divide the square into tenths to the east and to the north. There are a number of ways of doing this — you can buy a ready-made scale called a 'Romer'; most Silva compasses have the scale on the base; or you can make your own scale from a piece of card. So that you can get the idea we've put an 'overlay' on a part of our competition map (see Fig. 3).

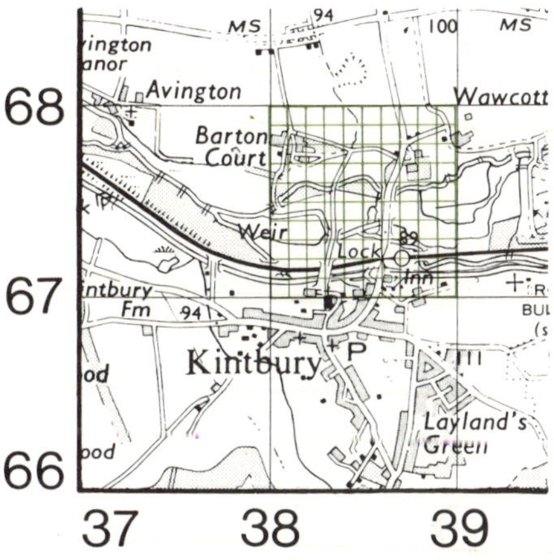


Part of 1:50 000 LANDRANGER, Sheet 174

Fig 3

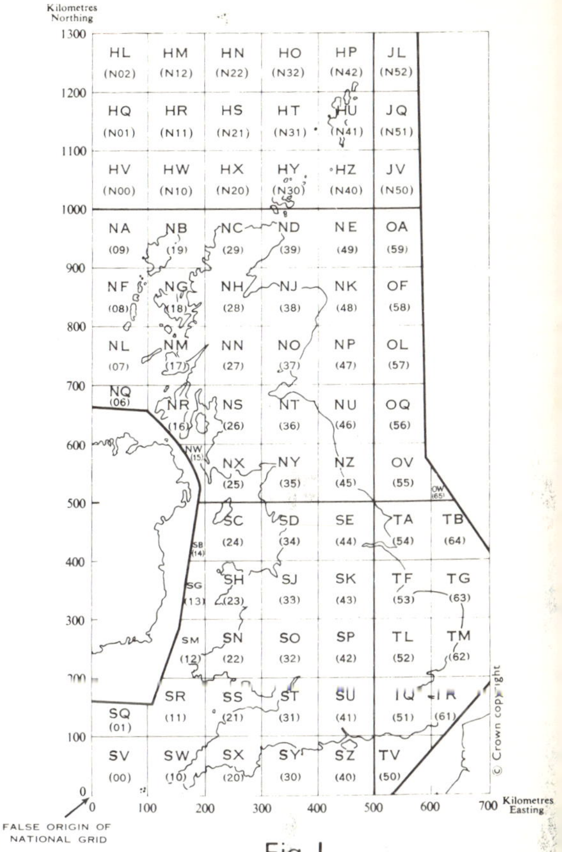


Fig 1

By applying this system to the station you'll find that it lies on the line 38.7 on the EASTING and 67.2 on the NORTHING. Thus the Grid Reference for Kintbury Station is 387672 on Landranger Sheet 174. With this reference anyone with the relevant map can locate the station to within 100 metres.

As long as you remember the E comes before N as EASTINGS came before NORTHINGS you can pin-point any place on any map, and you can use exactly the same reference on any scale of map or plan.

Now have a go at the competition on pages 48 and 49!

# Cracking the Code

To a postman, a postcode says a lot about you — not just the area in which you live or work, but the street, the group of houses or even the actual building. A complete postcode identifies a very small area — on average less than 15 houses. Cracking the code is easy. The first part represents the town or postcode district. The second part indicates in fine detail the section of that district where the mail is to be delivered, for example part of a street or even a single building.

(above)
A postman feeds letters into the segregator. Letters pass through the slits in the machine, separating them from the bulkier packages which have to be handled differently.

(left)
At the coding desk the postcode is 'translated' by the operator into a form which can be read by the automatic sorting machine. This 'language' takes the shape of small, luminescent dots in two rows.

(below)
Letters are removed from an automatic sorting machine. By 'reading' the postcode on the letters, this machine can sort them for up to 140 destinations at the rate of 16,000 an hour.

The postcode was designed so that the mail can be sorted by machine at every stage of its journey until it reaches the postman who makes the delivery. The combination of figures and letters in a postcode form a summary of the address which is easily converted to machine-readable language.

**Lines of dots**
When a letter bearing a postcode reaches the first sorting office, a machine-operator types the postcode — using a keyboard similar to that of a typewriter — and the machine translates it into two lines of dots on the envelope. One line corresponds to the first part of the postcode, the other line to the second part.

The first part, the 'outward' code, represents the distant sorting office to which the letter will be sent and from which it will be delivered. The second part of the postcode is called the 'inward' code and is used at the delivery office.

Sorting machines 'read' the line of dots corresponding to the outward code and sort the letter to the correct delivery office for that address. Once there, similar machines read the other line of dots and sort the letter right down to the postman who will deliver it.

**Improved version**

Postcodes are an essential part of plans to modernise the postal service and so keep down costs. They were introduced experimentally in the Norwich area in 1959. Technological developments, and experience at Norwich, led to an improved version which was introduced at Croydon towards the end of 1966. There are now 1½ million postcodes covering all 22 million addresses in the country.

**To use a postcode properly, always try to give it a line to itself at the end of the address. Always use block capitals, no punctuation and leave a space between the two parts of the code. A postcode should never be underlined.**

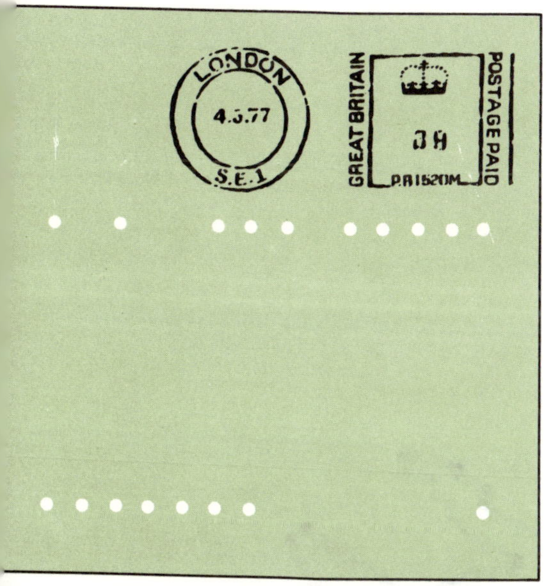


**Postcodes are translated into luminescent dots which are 'read' by sorting machines at speed.**

*Reproduced by courtesy of the Post Office Features and Information Bureau.*

# How Postcodes are Used

## THE OUTWARD CODE

For example, every postcode around Milton Keynes starts with the letters MK, and the complete outward code for a district of Bedford is MK42.

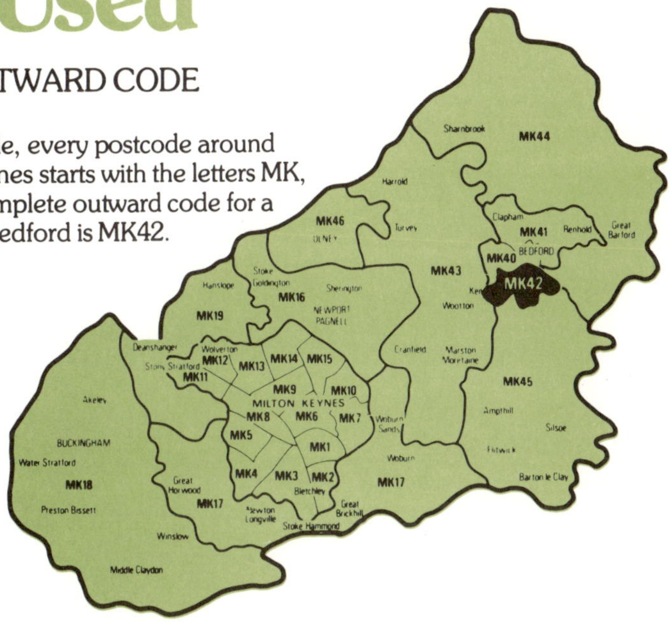


## THE INWARD CODE

Following our example MK42 is divided into sectors identified by figures.

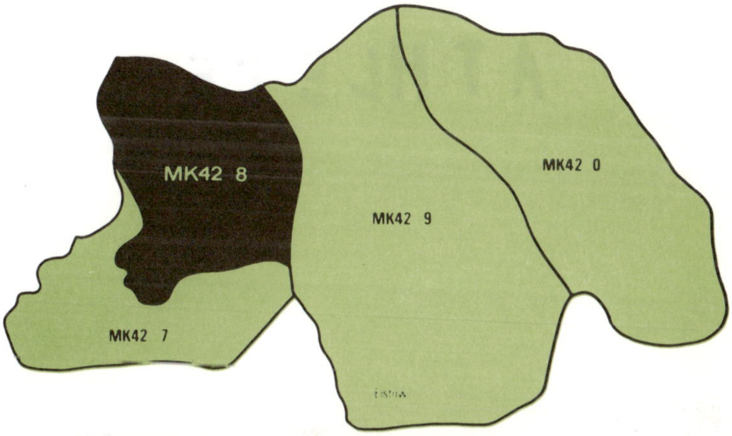


Each sector is divided into individual postcodes identified by letters.

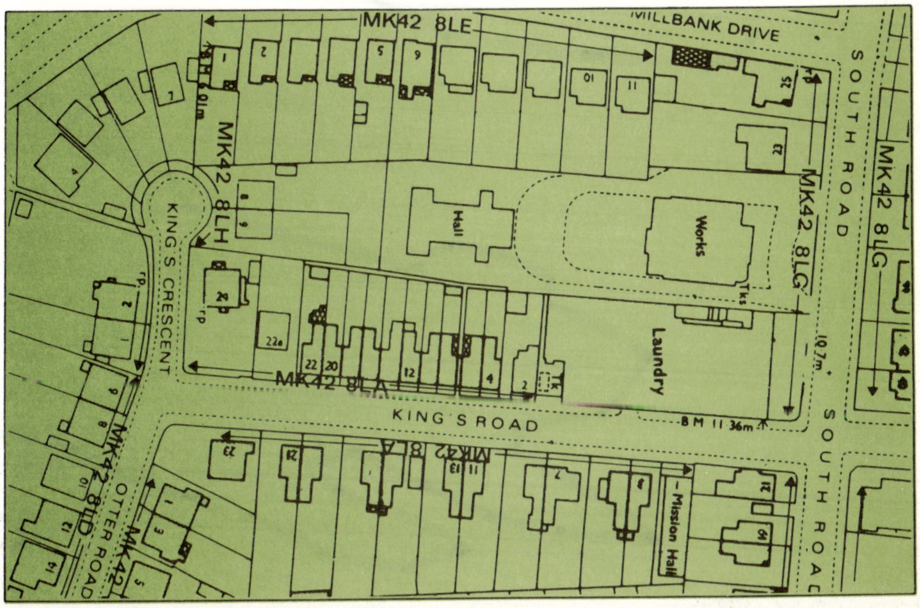

# THE PROFICIENCY BADGE PUZZLE SPREAD.

## SPOT THE BADGE HIDDEN IN THE LIMERICK!

ALL YOU HAVE TO DO IS FILL IN THE MISSING LETTERS TO FIND THE NAME OF A PROFICIENCY BADGE!

WHEN CUB SCOUTS ST_ND ROUND A FLAG POLE
__EY REMEMBER THE GREAT BADEN-POWELL
ONE _AD CALLED BERT
HAD A BADG_ ON HIS SHIR_
FOR MAKING A NOISE LIK_ AN OWL!

| A | T | H | L | E | T | E |
|---|---|---|---|---|---|---|

## SPOT THE ANIMALS!

HERE'S ONE FOR ANIMAL LOVERS. WE'VE DRAWN THE OUTLINES OF SEVERAL ANIMALS ON TOP OF EACH OTHER — HOW MANY ARE THERE AND WHAT ARE THEY?

## SAVE THE STRANDED CHILD!

ANYONE FOR THE RESCUER BADGE CAN YOU FIND YOUR WAY ACROSS THE RIVER WITHOUT CROSSING ANY BLACK LINES AND SAVE THE LITTLE GIRL WHO'S STRANDED ON THE OTHER SIDE?

Devised and drawn by Cliff Brown

## FIND THE TOOLS.

THESE LADS, WHO ALL HAVE THEIR HANDYMAN BADGE, HAVE BEEN INSTRUCTED TO BUILD A LOG CABIN IN THE WOODS BUT THEY'VE LOST THEIR TOOLS. CAN YOU FIND . . . 3 SAWS, 2 HAMMERS, 2 AXES, 2 'G' CLAMPS, PLIERS, A SCREWDRIVER, PINCHERS AND A CROWBAR? THEY ARE ALL HIDDEN IN THE PICTURE.

## WHAT SORT OF BADGE WOULD THIS PICTURE REPRESENT?

FILL IN ALL THE SHAPES WITH A DOT AND DISCOVER WHAT BADGE MIGHT BE REPRESENTED BY THE PICTURE.

HERE'S A PUZZLER FOR ALL FISHERMEN!

## WHO CAUGHT WHAT FISH?

check your answers on page 63

# A GIANT CROSSWORD

## CLUES ACROSS

1. Cloven-hoofed animals related to deer, goats and cattle (9)
6. You're doing one now! (9)
11. What you would be in old English (2)
12. Without a boy, ladle is masculine in French (2)
13. You'll find them joining bits of cloth (5)
15. To excite or stimulate (5)
18. It's said that ___ comes before beauty! (3)
20. It takes more than one to make a flower (5)
22. An island off the west coast of Scotland (5)
24. It used to be made from coal, now it's natural (3)
26. Lists of duties to be done in a particular order (5)

28/29. "To __, or not __ be" (Hamlet) (2, 2)

30. Fruit pies come from a mixed up start (5)
32. Not off! (2)
33. A person with a future has these, or someone searching for gold does this (9)
35. Not you! (2)
36. A pungent taste or smell (4)
37. A famous public school with tone (4)
38. Every cloud is said to have a silver one (6)
41. This is usually delivered from a pulpit (6)
43. It goes between bricks in a wall (6)
44. Removed the moisture from (5)
45. "One man ___ ___ dog" (3, 3)
46. A picturesque cave (5)
49. Meat sticks from splinters (5)
51. "___ ___ cry" (3, 3)
55. Wakes up (6)
56. Short-handled deep shovels for dipping up and carrying materials like flour, grain and coal (6)
57. Fruit like a lemon (4)
59. Type of paper from the desert? (4)
61. No backwards (2)
62. Tear up by the roots or get rid of (9)
65. The 'indefinite article' before a word beginning with a vowel (2)
66. This adjective describes oil in its natural state (5)
69. The same as 35 Across (2)
70. When you reach the bottom, it's the only way out (2)
71. Someone who refuses to believe in the goodness of human actions (5)
73. The winner of a track race did this (3)
74. They swivel in the air to show the wind's direction (5)
75. The name of the first Director-General of the BBC (5)
80. The insect from 1 Down (3)
81. Melody (5)
83. Vessels which float (5)
85. A unit of measure for printed matter (2)
86. The abbreviation which means 'in other words' (1, 1)
87. She was burnt at the stake (5, 4)
88. They add up to sixteen (3, 3, 3)

## CLUES DOWN

1. The region round the South Pole (9)
2. A pirate covers one with a patch (3)
3. Jumps (5)
4. A nuisance (4)
5. Many fish have these or you might weigh yourself on them! (6)
6. An assistant to a parish priest (6)
7. In cricket it takes six balls, and it's finished (4)
8. Slope (5)
10. You'll probably find some of these in a first aid kit (9)
13. Attacked (3, 2)
14. The same as 69 Across (2)
16. Feminine 'the' in French (2)
17. Another name for the Lesser White Heron (5)
19. Instruction from the lowest traffic light (2)
21. Be plentiful (6)
23. Swayed from side to side (6)
25. 'Twinkle, twinkle, little bat! How I wonder what you're __' (Lewis Carroll) (2)
27. Fish where two lines meet (5)
31. A patch is often used to make _ ____ in torn clothing (1, 4)
33. This often describes the luxury flat at the top of a block (9)
34. A method of signalling (9)
39. It's not out! (2)
40. Holds tightly (5)
41. Trousers, theatres and cinemas all have them (5)
42. The same as 32 Across (2)
46. A Scout award for gallantry with moderate risk (4, 5)
47. Direction of events towards the finish (5)
48. "__ and fro" (2)
49. "Open ______," said the robber (6)
50. You might do this to yourself if you fall over (6)
52. The same as 70 Across (2)
53. You write this at school (5)
54. Sherlock Holmes would have made one, and then taken it away, perhaps (9)
58. To get onto a horse (5)
60. Parts of a rupee (5)
63. A pattern on a piece of cloth (6)
64. These are never straight lines (6)
67. Abbreviation for Royal Academy (1, 1)
68. An important thing that happens (5)
71. It's made up of links (5)
72. The same as 39 Down (2)
75. He is, but I __ (2)
76. A famous Roman Emperor (4)
78. A wild goat of the Alps (4)
79. The same as 48 Down (2)
82. She lays eggs (3)
84. A shorter way of saying Edward (3)

check your answers on page 63

# The 1983 COMPETITION

## Find the answer to the question...

# Which way to Hop Castle?

**Prizes worth more than £450 to be won for you and your Pack**

Cub Scouts like being out and about. It's fun going on hikes and expeditions with your Six or the Pack. There's the thrill of exploring new places and discovering new things, the excitement of making journeys by different routes (even if they're only a short distance from home), and the enjoyment of having fun along the way with your friends.

The best hikes are usually those which are well planned. For Pack expeditions your Leaders will work out where you're going to go, and how you're going to get there . . . and back! Probably he will plan the route beforehand using a map. Now YOU have the chance to plan the route for an expedition using the map on the opposite page . . . and by entering the competition you could be one of the lucky Cubs to win a prize — and just look at the smashing prizes which Ordnance Survey are offering!

**This is the Background Story**

A Cub Scout Leader has planned to take the Pack on a hike one Saturday and, with the other Leaders, has worked out the route you will take. In the Pack Meetings before the great day, the Cubs have had map reading training sessions including finding specific points on a map using Grid References (or National Grid co-ordinates to give them their proper name). As a final 'test' the Leader gave each Cub a list of Grid References.

'We shall be going by the most direct route passing through these points,' the boys were told, 'BUT these references are *not* in the correct order. We shall start from the building on the outskirts of Kintbury at Grid Reference 376662 and finish at Hop Castle. I want you to find out where we'll be going, and to put the References in the order which will take us on the most direct route to the Castle. I have not given the Grid Reference for Hop Castle as I want you to work that one out for yourselves.'

The Leader gave each Cub a piece of paper with the following information:

| | | |
|---|---|---|
| **START** | **376662** | |
| | **423713** | |
| | **398694** | |
| | **440728** | |
| | **386675** | |
| | **394684** | |
| | **407706** | |
| **Hop Castle** | **?** | **FINISH** |

**Here's what YOU have to do**

1. Look at the map opposite and find each of the points given by the Grid References. Put the Grid References in an order which will give the *most direct* route between the start and Hop Castle. Work out the Grid Reference for Hop Castle.
2. On the Entry Form on page 61:
   a. Write the Grid References CLEARLY in their correct order in the appropriate boxes.
   b. Fill in your name, address, date of birth and Cub Scout Pack in BLOCK CAPITALS.
   c. Let us know which *three* items you most enjoyed in this Annual.
   d. Give us *two* ideas for items or features you would like to see in future Cub Scout Annuals.
3. Carefully cut out the Entry Form along the dotted line, and send it, to arrive not later than Monday, 31st January 1983 to:
   1983 Cub Scout Annual Competition,
   Editorial Department, The Scout Association,
   Baden-Powell House, Queen's Gate, LONDON
   SW7 5JS.

**The Rules**

1. All competitors must be under the age of 11 years on 31st December 1982.
2. The closing date for the competition is Monday, 31st January 1983.
3. All the entries will be placed in a sack. The FIRST PRIZE will be awarded to the first correct, complete entry drawn at a date to be arranged in February 1983. The Second Prize will be awarded to the second correct, complete entry to be drawn, and so on.
4. Prizewinners will be notified by post, and the full list of winners will be published in SCOUTING Magazine.
5. The first three prizewinners will be sent a copy of the Ordnance Survey catalogue from which they can choose what items they would like, up to the value of their prize.
6. All prizewinners will be sent a specially inscribed copy of the book Ordnance Survey Maps by J. B. Harley, and a further specially inscribed copy will be presented to his Pack.
7. The Editor's decision is final. No correspondence can be entered into, and entries cannot be returned.

**Remember! The Entry Form is on page 61!**

# THE PRIZES

**This year's competition is sponsored by Ordnance Survey**

## FIRST PRIZE

**£50** worth of Ordnance Survey products PLUS a copy of *Ordnance Survey Maps, A Descriptive Manual* by J.B. Harley (worth £7) for the winner PLUS a copy of the book for the winner's Pack.

## THIRD PRIZE

**£15** worth of Ordnance Survey products PLUS a copy of *Ordnance Survey Maps* PLUS a copy of the book for his Pack.

## SECOND PRIZE

**£25** worth of Ordnance Survey products PLUS a copy of *Ordnance Survey Maps* PLUS a copy of the book for his Pack.

## 25 RUNNERS-UP PRIZES

Each runner-up will receive a copy of *Ordnance Survey Maps* PLUS a copy of the book for his Pack.

Part of 1:50000 Landranger Sheet 174

# THE QUEEN'S BEASTS

**written and illustrated by Bill Bruce**

IF YOU WERE asked to name the Queen's Beasts you would probably start with corgis and horses, but the Queen has some more peculiar beasts than those . . . .

When Queen Elizabeth II was crowned in 1953, ten splendid heraldic beasts were made and were placed at the entrance to Westminster Abbey. The ten sculptures were of notable and honourable beasts, inherited from the Queen's ancestors and tracing the history of the British Royal Family.

The ten beasts and their histories are illustrated here . . . .

THE LION OF ENGLAND

THE GRIFFIN OF EDWARD III

THE YALE OF BEAUFORT

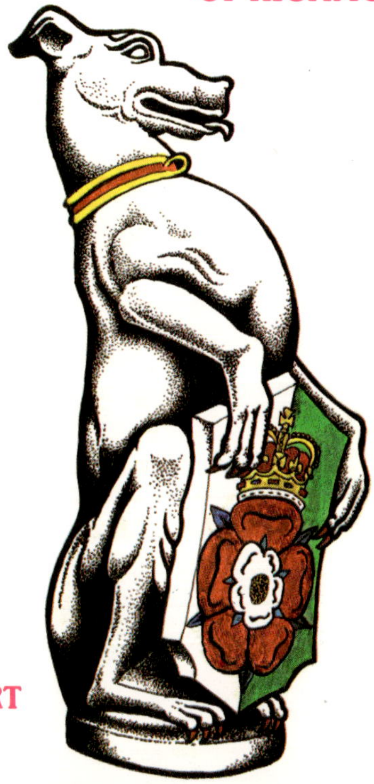

THE GREYHOUND OF RICHMOND

THE RED DRAGON OF WALES

THE FALCON OF THE PLANTAGENETS

THE BLACK BULL OF CLARENCE

THE WHITE LION OF MORTIMER

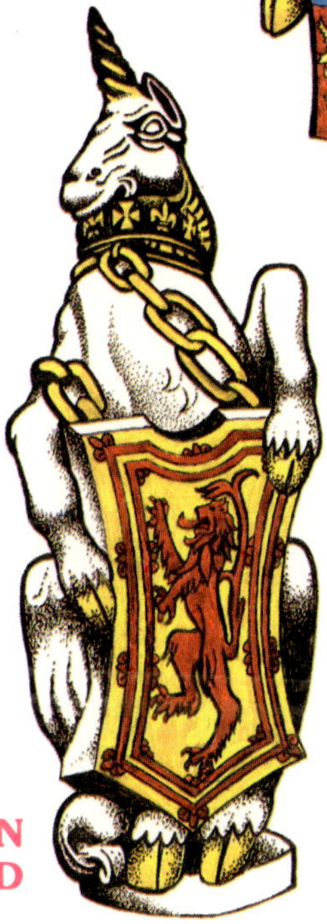

THE UNICORN OF SCOTLAND

THE WHITE HORSE OF HANOVER

**The Lion of England**

The golden Lion of England is the earliest of the royal beasts and holds the Royal Arms of the Queen. It symbolises the history of the monarchy of the country and is England's and Scotland's most important royal beast.

**The Griffin of Edward III**

The golden Griffin represents Edward III, who began the dynasties of York and Lancaster. The Griffin is an important beast which is half lion and half eagle and it holds the most recent of the royal badges, the badge of the House of Windsor. When King George V came to the throne he proclaimed that his Royal House should be called Windsor. In 1938, his son George VI instituted a badge for the newly-named House (which the Griffin is holding).

**The Falcon of the Plantagenets**

The silver Falcon of the Plantagenets was first used by Edward III, but it became a Yorkist creature which was often displayed within a golden fetterlock as shown in the badge that the Falcon is holding.

**The Black Bull of Clarence**

The Black Bull of Clarence was used as a badge by the Duke of Clarence, who was the second son of Edward III, ancestor of the House of York. The Bull is shown holding the royal arms as used from 1405 - 1603.

**The White Lion of Mortimer**

The White Lion of Mortimer depicts the Yorkist claim to the throne which came through the family of Mortimer and so the Lion is shown holding one of the Yorkist badges. The White Rose of York is shown against a sun which was the badge of Richard II who named Roger Mortimer as heir to the throne.

**The Yale of Beaufort**

The silver Yale of Beaufort commemorates the House of Lancaster and is shown holding a Beaufort badge which was adopted by Henry VII. The Yale is an heraldic antelope which is supposed to be able to swivel its horns to counter an attack from any side. It is shown with sharp tusks and usually has large gold spots on a silver background.

**The Greyhound of Richmond**

The white Greyhound of Richmond is shown holding a shield of the Tudor Rose badge. The Greyhound has been a popular royal beast with many of the Royal Houses since the time of Edward III.

**The Red Dragon of Wales**

The Red Dragon of Wales commemorates the union of the Houses of York and Lancaster which resulted in the House of Tudor. The Tudors were essentially Welsh and the Dragon is seen holding the arms of Llewelyn the Great who was recognised as the ruler of Wales. In 1911 these arms, with a coronet and the Royal Arms, were assigned to the Prince of Wales.

**The Unicorn of Scotland**

The white Unicorn of Scotland represents the Stuarts and is probably best known as one of the supporters of the Royal Arms of the United Kingdom. It is seen holding a shield of the old Royal Arms of Scotland.

**The White Horse of Hanover**

The White Horse of Hanover represents the House of Hanover and is seen holding a shield of the Royal Arms which was used from the accession of George I in 1714 until the union with Ireland in 1801.

# Who's got what?

**Designed by Malcolm Turner**
**Illustrated by Peter Harrison**

All the Cub Scout Proficiency Badges are on this page. We've given each of them a *number*. You'll also see 29 cartoons, each of which has a *letter*. What you have to do is to find which particular badge goes with which particular cartoon. (As far as the Athlete Badges are concerned, we've assumed that 5 points have been gained towards the Stage 1, 7 points towards Stage 2, and 10 points towards Stage 3).

What you do is this . . .

1. Write the numbers 1 to 29 down one side of a sheet of paper.
2. Identify the Badge.
3. Find the correct cartoon and write its letter beside the name of the Badge.

Here's the first one to give you a start . . .

1. SCIENTIST — Q

# WALES

## FOR CUB SCOUT OBSERVERS, COLLECTORS & EXPLORERS HERE ARE . . .

# ALL THE COUNTY BADGES OF THE UNITED KINGDOM

# NORTHERN IRELAND

**design and maps: Malcolm Turner**
**research: Gill Brackley**

As a Cub Scout you proudly wear badges on your uniform. Each badge lets people know something about you — the Arrow Badges and Proficiency Badges show your own achievements; your Group Nametape, District Badge and County Badge tells people where you do your Cub Scouting.

On this and the next three pages you'll find all the County Badges of The United Kingdom. There are many interesting things you can do with all this information (apart from just looking at how many County Badges there are!) For example . . . What's the origin of *your* County Badge? How many different County Badges can you see during 1983? (You could keep a record in this book). Be on the look-out for Scouts from other counties when you're on holiday or travelling about, or when Scouts from other parts of the country visit your neighbourhood. Start a collection of County Badges: ask your Cub Scout Leader if you can buy some 'spares' and keep them to swap with Cubs, Scouts, Venture Scouts and Leaders from other counties.

By the way, County Badges are sometimes changed. The ones illustrated here are correct at the time of going to press (December 1981). Also, please note that Scout Counties are not always the same as Local Government Counties in England, Wales and Northern Ireland, nor the Local Government Regions in Scotland.

1. Brecknock

2. Carmarthen

3. Ceredigion

4. Clwyd

5. Mid Glamorgan

6. South Glamorgan

7. West Glamorgan

8. Gwent

9. Gwynedd

10. Montgomery

11. Pembroke

12. Radnor

1. Antrim

2. Armagh

3. Belfast

4. Down

5. Fermanagh

7. Tyrone

6. Londonderry

1. Avon

2. Bedfordshire

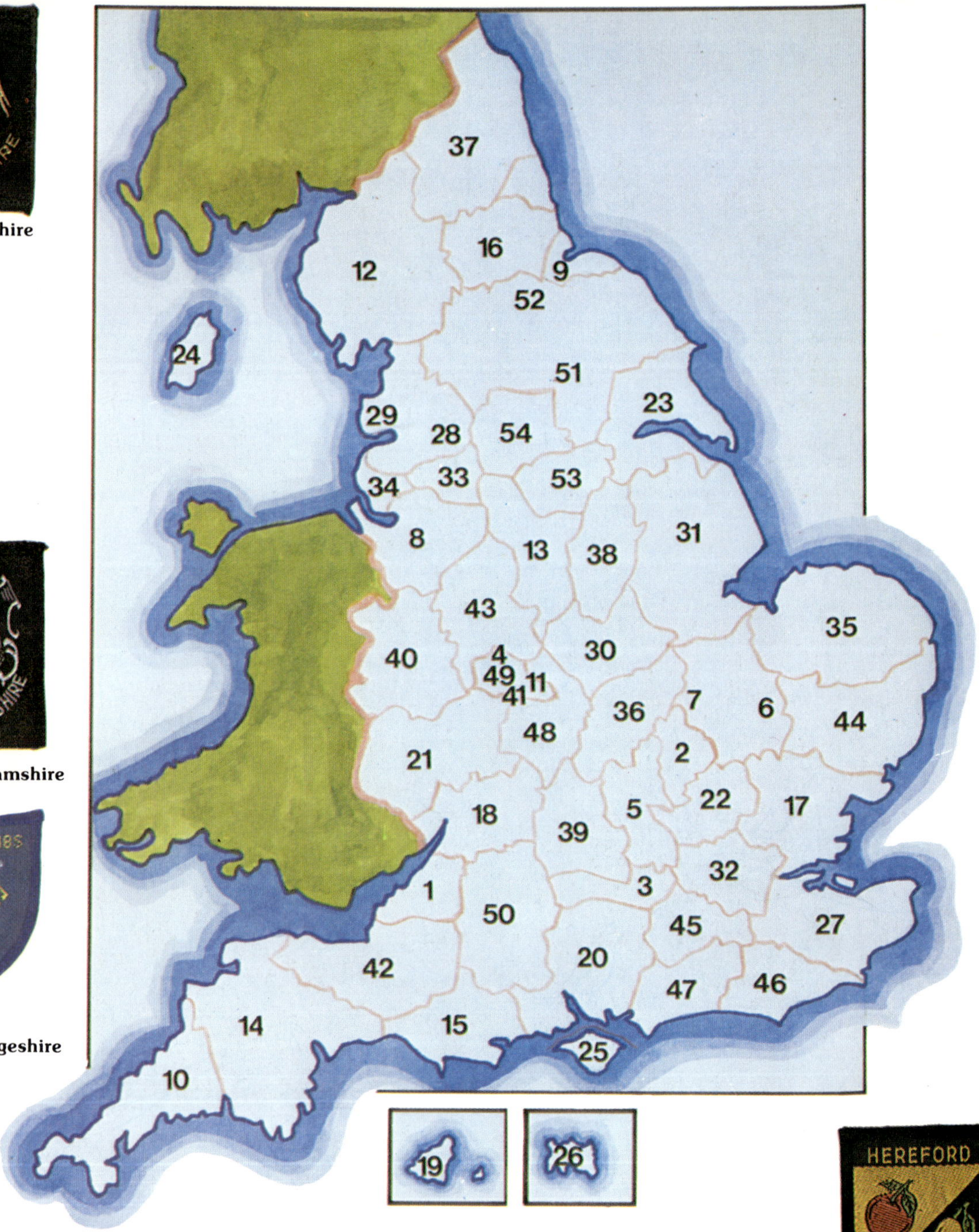

3. Berkshire

4. Birmingham

5. Buckinghamshire

6. East Cambridgeshire

7. West Cambridgeshire

8. Cheshire

21. Hereford and Worcester

9. Cleveland

10. Cornwall

13. Derbyshire

15. Dorset

17. Essex

19. Guernsey

22. Hertfordshire

11. Coventry

12. Cumbria

14. Devon

16. Durham

18. Gloucestershire

20. Hampshire

23. Humberside

# ENGLAND

24. Isle of Man

25. Isle of Wight

26. Jersey

27. Kent

28. East Lancashire

29. West Lancashire

30. Leicestershire

31. Lincolnshire

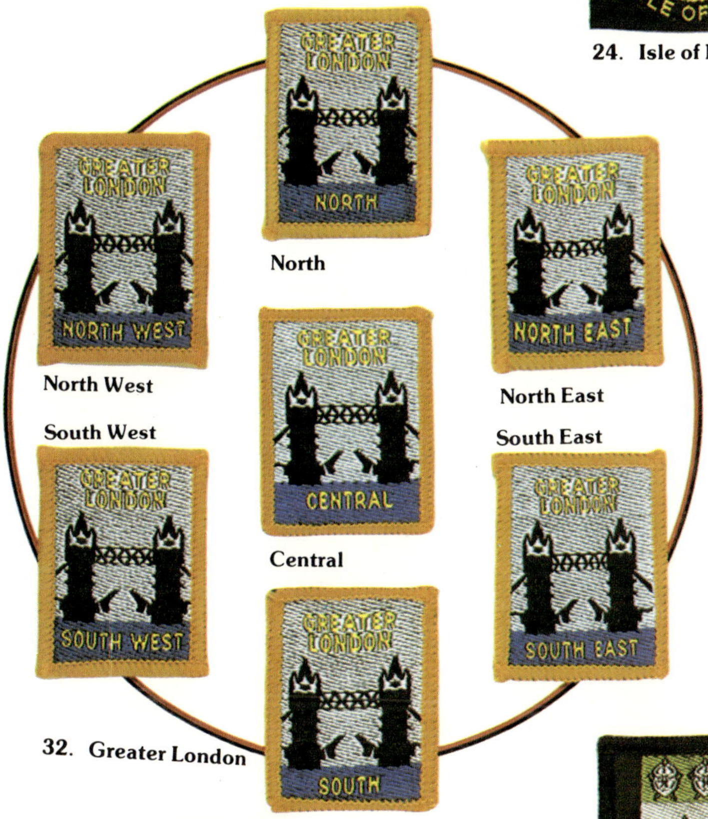

32. Greater London

33. Greater Manchester

34. Merseyside

35. Norfolk

36. Northamptonshire

37. Northumberland

38. Nottinghamshire

39. Oxfordshire

40. Shropshire

41. Solihull

42. Somerset

43. Staffordshire

44. Suffolk

45. Surrey

46. East Sussex

47. West Sussex

48. Warwickshire

49. West Mercia

50. Wiltshire

51. Central Yorkshire

52. North Yorkshire

53. South Yorkshire

54. West Yorkshire

# SCOTLAND

1. Aberdeen

2. Angus

3. Argyll North

4. Argyll South

5. Ayr

6. Banff and Buchan

7. Borders

8. Caithness

9. Clackmannan

10. Clydesdale

11. Dumfries

12. Dunbarton

13. Dundee

14. East Lothian

15. Edinburgh

16. Fife

17 Forth Valley

18. Gordon

19. Greater Glasgow

20. Inverness

21. Kincardine and Deeside

22. Midlothian

23. Moray

24. Orkney

25. Perth

25a. Kinross

26. Renfrew and Inverclyde

27. Ross and Sutherland

28. Shetland

29. Stewartry

30. Western Isles

31. West Lothian

32. Wigtown

# BE PREPARED
# Make an Emergency Map...Now!

The four main emergency services are the Police, the Fire Service, the Ambulance Service and the Coastguard. You may know how to make an emergency telephone call (if you don't it would be a good idea to find out) but, if you know where the emergency services are located in your area, you might save time by going direct to them rather than using the telephone: a delay of just 30 seconds could be a matter of life or death. A knowledge of the district round your home is essential if you are going to be able to make this decision in an emergency. There's also the point that, as a Cub, you should know your neighbourhood well anyway, so you can give clear answers to those who might ask for directions.

As far as the emergency services are concerned, you should know where the following are located:

**Doctors**
**Hospitals**
**Police stations and sub-stations**
**Fire stations and sub-stations**
**Public telephones**

*and, if you live near the coast . . .*

**Coastguard stations**

One way of getting the facts (and making sure that you remember them) is by making an *emergency map*.

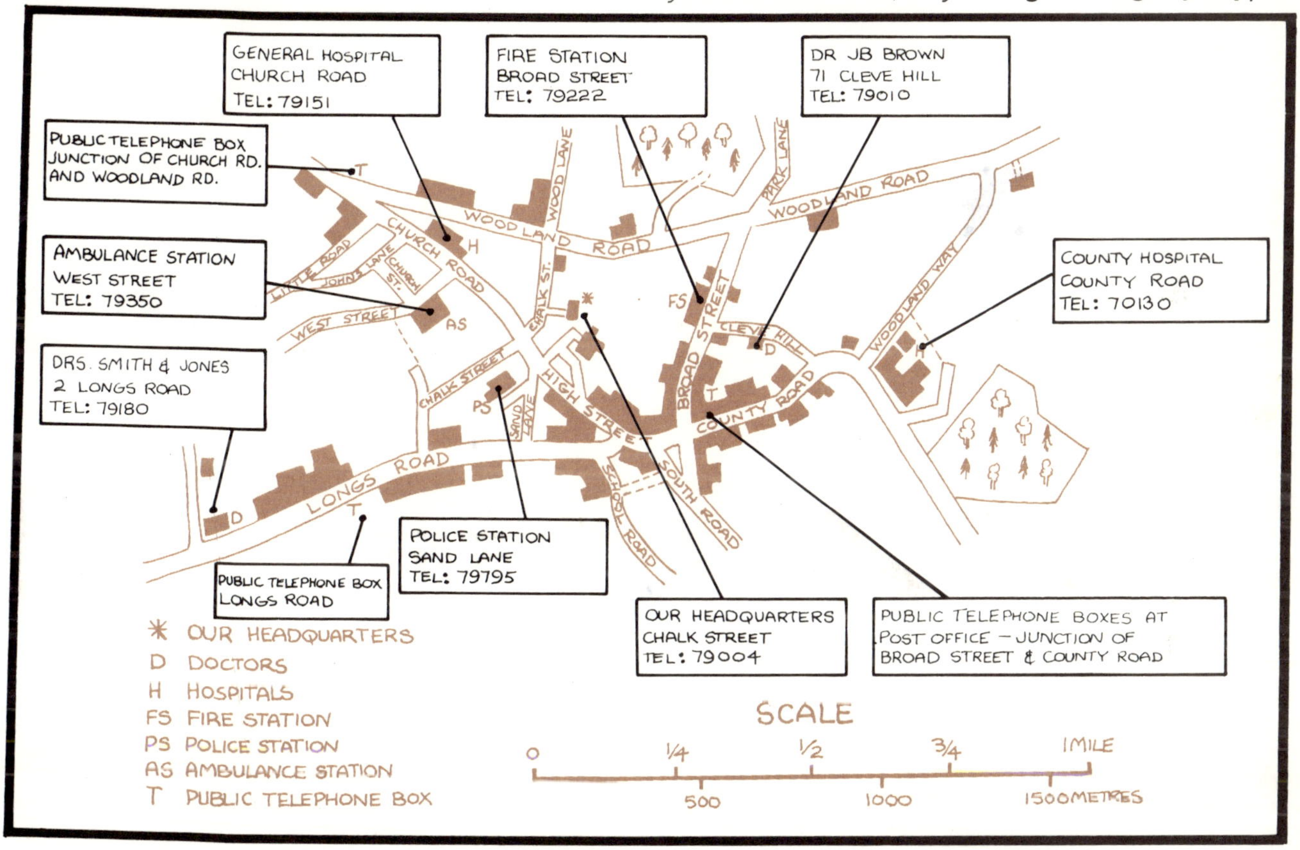


### Hints on making YOUR emergency map

1. MAKE SURE all the information on your map is accurate. Don't be tempted to draw your map from the comfort of an armchair at home, using the Town Guide, Ordnance Survey maps, and so on as your *only* sources of information, because some details in these publications may be out of date. Use them as a basis from which to work, but check by research on the ground by looking for yourself.

2. DON'T CLUTTER the map with *too* much detail which is not connected with the emergency services. Use *either* drawing pins with different coloured heads (or mapping pins) *or* a 'letter code' (as we have done in our illustration) to show the location of public telephones, doctors, etc. Don't forget to put a 'key' of what each represents on the map.

3. PUT THE FULL ADDRESS and telephone number of each 'emergency location' in panels round your map. Even better, put this information on self-adhesive labels on a transparent overlay with a leader line from each panel to the location to which it refers. If you do this on the overlay, you can make changes without having to re-draw the map.

4. DON'T THINK that when you've finished your map you can leave it to gather dust for months or even years! It is not a pretty picture to be admired from a distance. It's an important piece of equipment and needs to be looked after. It will get out of date as doctors move, telephone boxes are removed or installed, etc. Make it YOUR job — yes, *your* job — to keep your eyes and ears open for any changes which take place and then make the necessary amendments to the map straight away.

# JET BOAT

*DRIVEN BY HOT-AIR PROPULSION*

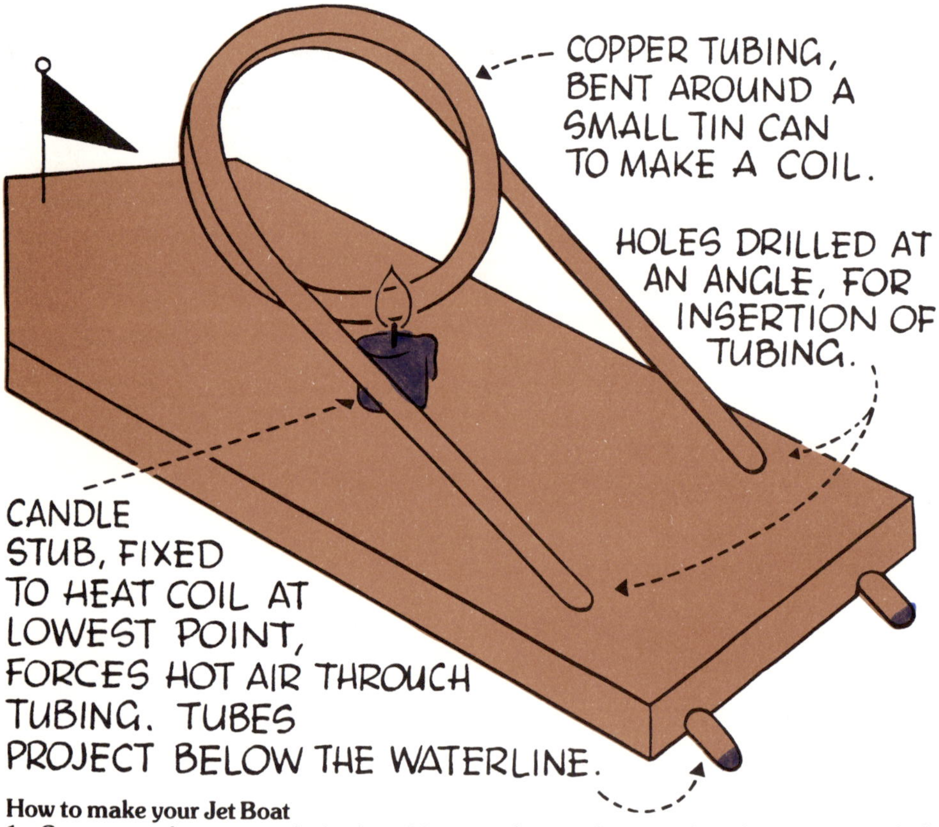


**How to make your Jet Boat**

1. Cut a piece of scrap pine plank, about 30cm long and 10cm wide, and saw a pointed bow at one end.
2. Procure a piece of copper tubing about 50cm long and about 1cm in diameter; try your local garage or motorcar scrapyard. At its centre, bend the tubing around some cylindrical object such as a small tin can, to make a coil as shown in the sketch.
3. Drill two holes at an angle in the stern of the boat, as illustrated — diameter of holes according to the diameter of the tubing.
4. Insert the tubing into the holes, so that about 2cm of the tubing projects below the water line.
5. On the point of a nail driven into the board from underneath, fix a stub of candle so that the candle flame, when lit, will heat the lowest part of the coil.

**Operating your Jet Boat**

Hold the boat bow downwards, and fill the tubing with water. A lot of water will run out when you right the boat again, but an adequate quantity of water will remain in the coil to run the boat for a couple of minutes.

Place the boat in the water, and light the candle. After a minute or two the jet engine will start working, as hot air is forced out of one end of the tubing, and drives the boat forward.

For even more jet power, use two candle stubs side by side, so that the flames heat the lowest part of the coil.

## BEAN-BAG TOSS

**TARGET:**

Cut a 24cm radius circle from scrap hardboard or other suitable material. Sandpaper the edge. Paint the board a light colour so that the markings will show up well, using a durable paint. Around the circumference mark a point every 60°, using a protractor, and rule lines from these six points to the centre. Then use durable black paint to paint in the lines and the numbers as shown in the sketch. Also paint the tin and, when the paint is dry, paint on the number 100. Then bolt the tin can to the centre of the board, using washers to hold it firmly. The tin can should be a **shallow** one, some 10cm in diameter, such as a shallow fish can.

**BEAN-BAGS:**

Make 5 small bean-bags about 7cm x 7cm square from any cloth oddments. Fill each bag fairly loosely with dried beans, before finally sewing up.

**RULES:**

1. To set up the pitch, place the target board on the ground and mark or chalk a circle around the target on the ground — 3 metres radius. This is the throwing-line. (If played on lawn, put 6 pegs in the ground opposite the lines on the board, and 3 metres from the centre, to denote throwing-line).
2. In turn, each player takes the 5 bean-bags and, toeing the circular throwing line at any desired place, tosses the bags at the target. The object is (a) to get the bags into the can and (b) score in the numbered areas around the can.
3. When a bag lands in the can the player adds 100 to his score, and also wins an extra throw — removing the bag from the can for his extra throw.
4. To score on the board itself, a bag must be completely inside a numbered area — not touching a line or hanging over the edge.
5. A match consists of three alternate innings of 5 throws per player, the highest score for all three innings being the winner. You can play singles matches between two players, or make up competing teams.

## A STARSCOPE

MAKE IT FROM A LARGE PLASTIC BOTTLE. CUT SLOTS EACH SIDE, NEAR BOTTOM, TO TAKE SLIDES MADE FROM THIN BLACK-PAINTED CARD.

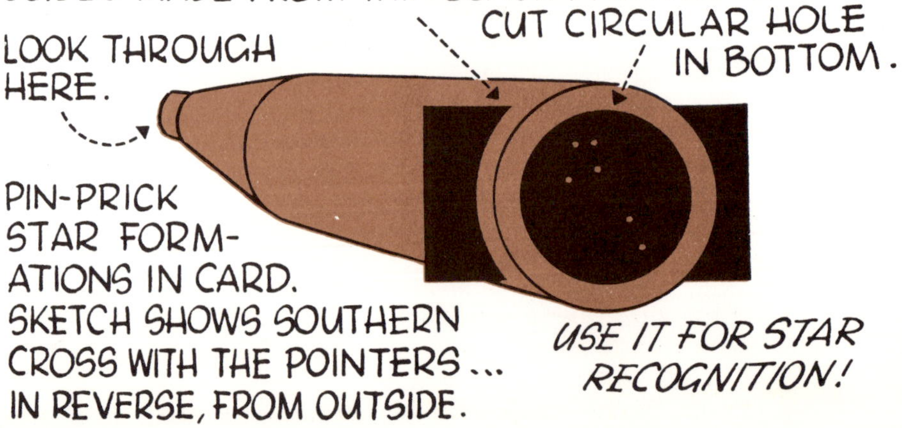

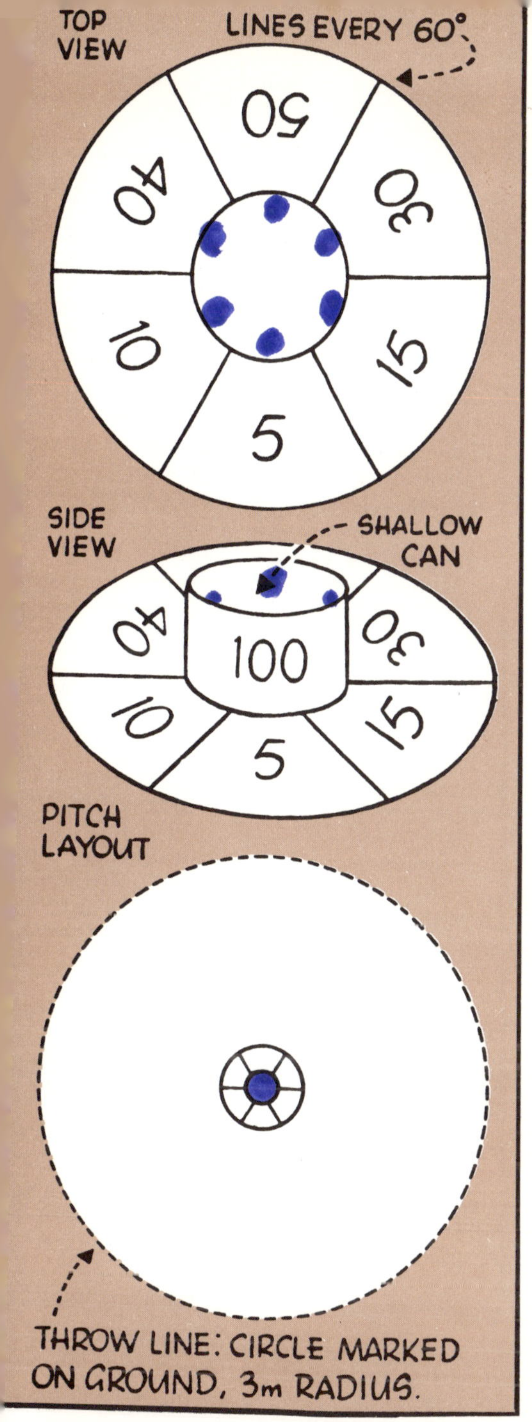


# FLASHCARDS

A VISUAL TRAINING MEDIUM, MADE FROM SCRAP CARD. MAKE CARDS ABOUT 7cm SQUARE*... A SET FOR EACH SUBJECT...FOR RECOGNITION EXERCISES... MAP SIGNS, TRAIL SIGNS, TRACKS, FLAGS, LEAVES, STARS, BOATS, AIRCRAFT, ANIMALS, BIRDS, ETC.

* OR LARGER

ONE SIDE OF A CARD SHOWS ILLUSTRATION, THE REVERSE SIDE GIVES THE DESCRIPTION

*TRAINING GAME*: *PLACE PACK OF FLASHCARDS ON A TABLE, ILLUSTRATIONS FACE-UP. PLAYERS SIT AROUND. IN TURN, EACH PLAYER PICKS UP TOP CARD AND CALLS OUT IDENTIFICATION. IF HE FAILS, THE NEXT PLAYER HAS A TRY. EACH PLAYER KEEPS THE CARDS HE HAS IDENTIFIED, FOR SCORING PURPOSES AFTER GAME.*

THE SCOPE IS ALMOST LIMITLESS...

# AMBUSH

A "STALKING" GAME, ON A BOARD ABOUT 20cm SQUARE

This "stalking" game for two players is very simple to make, but challenging to play. Two players take part.

**EQUIPMENT**

**BOARD:**

Cut a piece of scrap cardboard or other suitable material, 20cm square. Mark out the diagram as shown in the sketch.

**COUNTERS:**

You need two counters or "men" of one colour, and two of another colour. Use cutout cardboard discs, or bottletops, or buttons, etc.

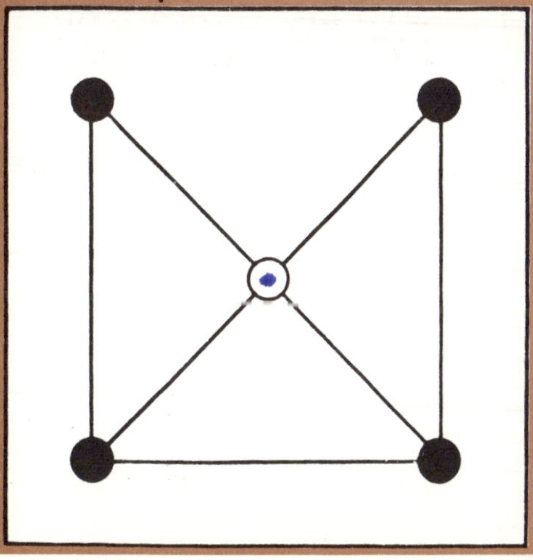

**RULES:**

1. The first player places his two men on the two top spots, and the other player puts his two men on the two button spots. The centre spot remains empty.
2. The player at the top starts the game by moving one of his men to the centre spot. His opponent then moves one of his men to the space vacated. Taking alternate turns, the players continue in this fashion.
3. No "jumping" is permitted. Moves must always be along one of the lines, from one spot to an adjacent empty spot.
4. The winner is the one who corners or "ambushes" his opponent's men, so that neither can be moved.

# The 1981 Competition WINNERS

Not three, but SIX cheers for British Rail! We certainly had lots of entries for our 1981 competition. It was quite a difficult one, and the prizes donated by British Rail were fantastic — a total of six free unlimited mileage journeys for the prizewinners and two adults. For those of you who didn't get the 1981 Annual (or who got it, but have forgotten what the competition was about), readers had to identify eight places from photographs and state in which British Rail Region each was located. We sorted out all the correct entries, put them in a bag and went along to Paddington Station, London, where Bill Dorrington, the driver of the 11.25 Cornish Riviera Express drew the winners.

**Christopher Davies in Glasgow where he went on one of his prizewinning journeys.**

## FIRST PRIZE

CHRISTOPHER DAVIES (2nd Colwyn Bay, 1st Mochdre Pack, North Wales)
Christopher won three unlimited rail journeys for himself and his parents. At the time of the competition he was 10 and had been a Cub for two years. "We live over our newsagents and grocery shop in Colwyn Bay," he wrote. "I have a younger brother called Jonathan who is nine. We both go to the Ysgol Cystennin Junior School and are both Cubs." According to his mother Christopher is, "mad keen on trains and used to spend a lot of time train spotting." His other interests include photography and watching television, and he always enjoys going to the family's caravan on a farm near his home.

His first rail journey took him (and his parents and Jonathan) on a day trip to London on the hottest day of 1981. He wanted to see the pigeons in Trafalgar Square, watch (and hear) Big Ben strike mid-day, visit the London Transport Museum at Clapham, go to Hamley's toy shop and listen to a band in St. James's Park — they did the lot! For the second trip the Davies family had a day trip to Cardiff, and for the third they visited relations in Glasgow for a few days.

**David Cook, who won the second prize.**

## SECOND PRIZE

DAVID COOK (20th Sheffield 'A' Pack)
David joined Cubs on the 8th September 1980, the day after his eighth birthday. He reckons his Pack, "is the best in the City." He goes to Ecclesall Church of England Junior School which is connected to the same church as his Pack (one of three Packs in the 20th Sheffield Group). He likes swimming, cycling, sailing and reading. With his parents and younger brother, Simon, he decided he wanted to go to John o' Groats for the first free trip. The family took the train to Thurso, went by bus to John o' Groats and then took the ferry to the Orkneys. On their way up and down Scotland they stopped over at Edinburgh, Aviemore, Inverness, Carbisdale Castle and Pitlochry, staying in Youth Hostels. For his second journey, David hopes to take his family either to Scotland again or to Jersey.

## THIRD PRIZE

CHRISTOPHER FAZEY (2nd Haxby and Wigginton Thursday Pack, York)
Christopher took a few weeks to write and tell us a bit about himself because he broke his arm just after he received our letter telling him of his prize. Anyway, he's been an active Cub for some time, has several Proficiency Badges and has been on Pack holidays. His older sister is a Guide. He enjoys cycling, walking and stamp collecting. In September 1981 Christopher wrote and told us that he'd be using his free trip to bring his parents to London. "We shall be staying at Baden-Powell House," he said. "I'd like to go to the Natural History and Science Museums, and to The Tower of London."

As Chris had said he'd be at B.-P. House I dropped a line to the Editorial Department at Scout HQ and asked, "Could a surprise be arranged for him?"

**Christopher Fazey, who won the third prize, with Paul Daniels.**

Well, we could write a full feature on what happened to Chris, but there just isn't space. One thing led to another. Seats for Paul Daniels' show *It's Magic* were booked: Mr. and Mrs. Fazey knew, but Chris didn't. So he wondered what was happening when he (and his Mum and Dad) were whisked away in a taxi. Chris was delighted when he heard where they were going, and the whole show was great. But there was one more surprise which none of the Fazeys knew about. After the show they were led out of the theatre, through the stage door, up a flight of winding stairs and into Paul Daniels' dressing room! Paul Daniels gave Chris a warm welcome and showed him a few tricks as well as some of his props. A very tired Cub Scout went back to Baden-Powell House that night . . . .

# THE CUT-OUT PAGE!

We've designed this page of your Annual this year so you can do four things for the price of one stamp (your postage to us). Using the forms on this page you can 1) enter the competition, 2) apply for a FREE Nuts of the World Wallchart, 3) send in a photograph for the SNAP IT! Challenge, and 4) join in our Stamps for Lifeboats appeal. You do *not* have to enter all four — it's up to you whether you use one, two, three, or all four. However, *please* fill in all the parts of the forms you do use in BLOCK CAPITALS, so we can read them! By the way, if you haven't got a photograph for the SNAP IT! Challenge before the 31st January 1983, keep that entry form until you have!

Cut out the forms you use, put them in one envelope — we'll sort them out when we get them — and address the envelope to: Cub Scout Annual, Editorial Department, The Scout Association, Baden-Powell House, Queen's Gate, London SW7 5JS.

P.S. We hope you'll read the other side of this page before you cut it up, as it gives you an idea of what's in store in the 1984 Cub Scout Annual. Make sure you're one of the first to order YOUR OWN copy — the sooner the better!

cut carefully along this line

## WHICH WAY TO HOP CASTLE? (see page 48)

**Competition Entry Form**

To: Cub Scout Annual, Editorial Dept., Baden-Powell House, Queen's Gate, London SW7 5JS.
PLEASE COMPLETE THIS FORM IN BLOCK CAPITALS

NAME ______

ADDRESS ______

______

______

Cub Scout Pack ______

Date of Birth ______

*Please complete this section as well:*
The three items I enjoyed most in the 1983 Cub Scout Annual were:

1. ______
2. ______
3. ______

I would like to make these suggestions for features in a future Cub Scout Annual.

1. ______
2. ______

**CLOSING DATE 31 JANUARY 1983**

**The most direct route to Hop Castle is:**

(Please write numbers clearly)

| START POINT | 3 | 7 | 6 | 6 | 6 | 2 |
|---|---|---|---|---|---|---|
| Second Grid Ref. Point | | | | | | |
| Third Grid Ref. Point | | | | | | |
| Fourth Grid Ref. Point | | | | | | |
| Fifth Grid Ref. Point | | | | | | |
| Sixth Grid Ref. Point | | | | | | |
| Seventh Grid Ref. Point | | | | | | |
| The Grid Reference of Hop Castle is | | | | | | |

cut carefully along this line

## FREE OFFER Nuts of the World Wallchart

**CLOSING DATE 31 JANUARY 1983**

(see page 2)

Please put this form into the hat and if mine is one of the first 50 to be drawn please send me a FREE wallchart.

NAME ______

ADDRESS ______

______

Fill in your name and address HERE and HERE

**ADDRESS LABEL**

______

______

______

______

______

From: Editorial Dept., Baden-Powell House, London SW7 5JS.

cut carefully along this line

cut carefully along this line

## SNAP IT! CHALLENGE

(see page 2)

**CLOSING DATE 30 JUNE 1983**

To: Cub Scout Annual, Editorial Dept., Baden-Powell House, Queen's Gate, London SW7 5JS.
*Attach this form to the back of your photograph.*

I took this photograph myself. ______

The caption/title of the photograph is

______

______

FROM
NAME ______

ADDRESS ______

______

cut carefully along this line

## STAMPS FOR LIFEBOATS

**CLOSING DATE 31 JANUARY 1983**

(see page 2)

These stamps are to go towards the 1983 Cub Scout Annual unused Stamps for Lifeboats project.

stick corner of stamp only

stick corner of stamp only

FROM
NAME ______

ADDRESS ______

______

# Your 1984 Cub Scout Annual is being prepared!

## These are just a few samples of the many items you'll find in its 64 action-packed pages...

When you're a SCOUT... What you can look forward to when you go up into the Scout Section

A FABULOUS COMPETITION with great prizes

An exciting adventure story

LET'S GO EXPLORING!

The history of THE AMERICAN COWBOY

Fascinating Facts of Nature

Our special 'Behind the Scenes' feature is still a SECRET!

CROSSWORDS

**CLiFF BROWN has devised four puzzle pages**

# Make sure YOU are prepared!

## Order your own copy of the Annual early!